C000078407

THE WORDS \

THE WORDS WILL COME

New Plays from the RADA Elders Company

Broken Pieces

Our Father

The Word

Down the Hatch

Of Blood

OBERON BOOKS
LONDON

WWW.OBERONBOOKS.COM

First published in 2018 by Oberon Books Ltd
521 Caledonian Road, London N7 9RH
Tel: +44 (0) 20 7607 3637 / Fax: +44 (0) 20 7607 3629
e-mail: info@oberonbooks.com
www.oberonbooks.com

10 9 8 7 6 5 4 3 2 1

Editorial copyright © Vivian Munn, 2018

Vivian Munn is hereby identified as editor of this collection
in accordance with section 77 of the Copyright, Designs and Patents
Act 1988. The editor has asserted his moral rights.

Broken Pieces © A. C. Smith, 2014

Our Father © Deborah Bruce, 2015

The Word © Nell Leyshon, 2016

Down the Hatch © Frances Poet, 2017

Of Blood © Christopher William Hill, 2018

The authors are hereby identified as authors of their contributions in
accordance with section 77 of the Copyright, Designs and Patents Act
1988. The authors have asserted their moral rights.

All rights whatsoever in this play are strictly reserved and application for
performance etc. should be made before commencement of rehearsal to
the Authors' agents, as indicated within each play. No performance may
be given unless a licence has been obtained, and no alterations may be
made in the title or the text of the play without the author's prior written
consent.

You may not copy, store, distribute, transmit, reproduce or otherwise
make available this publication (or any part of it) in any form, or
binding or by any means (print, electronic, digital, optical, mechanical,
photocopying, recording or otherwise), without the prior written
permission of the publisher.

A catalogue record for this book is available from the British Library.

PB ISBN: 9781786825841
E ISBN: 9781786825858

Printed and bound by 4EDGE Limited, Hockley, Essex, UK.
eBook conversion by Lapiz Digital Services, India.

Visit www.oberonbooks.com to read more about all our books and to buy them. You will
also find features, author interviews and news of any author events, and you can sign up for
e-newsletters so that you're always first to hear about our new releases.

Printed on FSC® accredited paper

This anthology is dedicated to my mother

Elsa A Munn

*whose unswerving faith in the work
inspires me to persevere*

Contents

Introduction

The RADA Elders Company was conceived by Joan Oliver, RADA's then Education & Outreach Manager, as an opportunity for older people to experience the academy's training at its best. It was thanks to Joan's tenacity, and funding from ICAP, that classes were able to begin in 2013. The desire was to create a company in which the contributors felt unpatronised, and were able to experience a wide range of theatre disciplines and skills.

The course challenges the perceptions of what an older generation can achieve. It is not only a great chance to socialise, interact and make new friends, but also a very serious attempt to develop performing skills. The students that audition come from diverse backgrounds, and acting ability is, by no means, the sole criterion for gaining a place in the company. Students attend a variety of classes, including Voice, Movement, Singing, Alexander Technique, Animal Study, Meisner, and workshops in Classical and Contemporary Acting. At the conclusion of the course, public performances of a play specially written for them are given in a RADA theatre. For many, the programme is full of new experiences: clearly, they are re-energized, re-invigorated and often re-invent themselves along the way.

Each year a playwright is invited to create a piece with equal parts for the sixteen actors. The writer has unlimited access to the classroom, sometimes observing improvisations on a suggested theme; and this unique opportunity has been a valuable learning experience for the company. The five plays in this anthology are timeless offerings, and while specifically written with an older age group in mind, their performance is not restrictive. The material is unique, and will be extremely useful for any Elders group seeking a selection of dynamic and thought-provoking works. They are challenging pieces which have sparked lively debate within the RADA Elders Company; and I hope these stimulating scripts will inspire new productions by other Elders groups.

I would like to take this opportunity to thank the playwrights for their commitment to the project; Joan Oliver for her original vision and encouragement; Carys Williams, RADA's first Widening Participation and Outreach Manager, for her dedication and tireless promotion of this extremely vital work; and the entire team of devoted RADA staff. The RADA Elders Company currently receives the support of The Austin and Hope Pilkington Trust and several anonymous donors.

Vivian Munn
Director, RADA Elders Company
September 2018

Broken Pieces by A. C. Smith

When experiences are too painful to remember, sometimes it's easier to forget.

Archaeologist Barbara's world has been turned upside down by the loss of her husband Harold: her partner both in work and in life. In her efforts to cope, she has withdrawn from these painful memories, but the only way she can become whole again is by facing them. *Broken Pieces* chronicles Barbara's bittersweet process of remembering – tracing backwards through time to reclaim and honour both her own experience and the great love of her life.

'The past never really goes away. It just gets buried a little deeper.'

Our Father by Deborah Bruce

London, 2015. George Parish, 'a national treasure' and hugely respected television broadcaster, has died.

His children return to the family home to support each other and make plans for the funeral, as reporters gather outside.

On the other side of the city, three siblings are threatened with eviction from the house they have lived in all their lives; and an actress takes to her bed to mourn the loss of her lover.

How has the death of this public figure set in motion a sequence of events that explore legacy and inheritance? And what do we leave behind for others to live with, when we are gone?

The Word by Nell Leyshon

Suburban London. A street with houses, flats, a church and a doctor's surgery.

Eva finds that she is having problems with her words: they are replaced, or they won't come. Concerns about a stroke or dementia are forgotten when she speaks to others in the street and they find they have the same problem.

How will they be cured? By the priest or by the doctor?

The Word is about illness and cure. It is about our own relationship with the words we use, and how they affect our identity.

Down the Hatch by Frances Poet

Ancient and aloof, Edward has gathered his family together for a meal in a Highland retreat, but nobody seems to know why. A former submariner, Edward has spent his life battening down the hatches, rarely emerging to communicate with his family, and consequently the group he has assembled are ill at ease together. This explosive group of people include: his ice-cold daughter who hates her step mother, his son's ex-wife and his new gay partner, warring former cleaners, and a waitress who reminds all the guests of Edward's late first wife. When Edward finally arrives late to his own party, the group are shocked to discover a recent stroke has left communication physically impossible. With the help of his enigmatic nurse, who acts as translator, Edward makes a toast that none of his family were expecting.

Down the Hatch is a pitch black comedy about the need to let out our repressed selves and show the world who we really are.

Of Blood by Christopher William Hill

Within the walls of a remote castle, cut off from the outside world by a vast forest, an ancient countess and her servants enact rituals that echo a violent and long-ago past. The arrival of Katalin, a peasant woman from the mountains, brings new blood to the dusty household and reawakens the darkest of carnal desires.

Inspired by the legend of the vampire Elizabeth Báthory, *Of Blood* is a tale of love and lust and the lengths to which we might go in order to arrest the transience of youth.

BROKEN PIECES
by A.C. Smith

All rights whatsoever in this play are strictly reserved and application for performance etc. should be made before rehearsal to Berlin Associates, 7 Tyers Gate, London SE1 3HX. No performance may be given unless a licence has been obtained.

Characters

BARBARA – Archaeologist
HAROLD – Archaeologist, Barbara's husband
FLORENCE – Old friend of Barbara's
ROGER – University Dean
NEWSREADER

Memory site:
EVE – Lead Archaeologist
CATHERINE – Archaeologist, Eve's Deputy, Finds Manager
EMILY – Excavation Team Member, Geoarchaeology
Specialist
JOHN – Excavation Team Member, Archaeo-Engineer
JOANNA – Volunteer Excavation Team Member
MARY – Volunteer Excavation Team Member

The alto section:
SHARON
JOYCE
ANNE
JULIE

Egypt site:
MAGGIE – Archaeologist
LOU – Archaeologist
FRANK – Excavation Team Member
HELEN – Excavation Team Member

MEMBERS OF THE ENSEMBLE
can play additional roles as various members of
the excavation teams.

SETTINGS – TIME AND PLACE

The play begins in 2014 and moves backwards in time covering a period of fifty years, however the majority of the play's action is concentrated in 2011. The play's locations include:

Barbara's Dream World
Barbara's Home
Barbara's Memory Site / Eve & Catherine's Dig
Roger's Office
Harold's Egyptian Site
Barbara And Florence's Student Flat
University Party

A NOTE FROM THE PLAYWRIGHT

Broken Pieces is set in two connected but separate worlds: Barbara's conscious reality and the memory site of her unconscious mind. Props can pass between worlds (and events cause repercussions that manifest physically across the border), but characters are unable to see others who are not in their 'world' and do not interact with them, until the play's final moments.

It is critical that the audience quickly realises that the action of the play takes place in reverse.

The set should ideally include a display where the timeline events can be noted.

The sense of moving back in time can also be reinforced by directorial choices that give a sense of rewinding, moving backwards, or going deeper. The scene changes may be as important as the scenes in achieving this.

The memory site team should handle all objects and props they encounter as fascinating archaeological objects, no matter how mundane they may seem.

Broken Pieces was first performed in the GBS Theatre at RADA on Saturday 13 December 2014.

DIRECTOR – Vivian Munn
DESIGNER – Miguel Guzman
MOVEMENT DIRECTOR – Angela Gasparetto
VOICE TUTOR – Caroline Kilpatrick
SINGING TUTOR – Helen Chadwick
SUPPORT TUTOR – Ingrid Schiller

Cast
BARBARA – Shirley Bracewell
HAROLD – Donald Elliot
EVE – Ruth Steele
CATHERINE – Yvonne Levy
EMILY – Pam Zinkin
JOHN – Kenneth Beasley
JOANNA – Maria Hatzipetrou rozou
MARY – Sandie Barwick
FLORENCE – Jenni Wredden
ROGER – Damian Murphy
SHARON – Judith Bevan
JOYCE – Sandie Barwick
ANNE – Pam Zinkin
JULIE – Vivienne Cove
MAGGIE – Belinda Milani
LOU – Jacqui Holder
FRANK – Damian Murphy
HELEN – Maria Hatzipetrou rozou
NEWSREADER – Belinda Milani

Production Team
STAGE MANAGER – Josh Chalk
DEPUTY STAGE MANAGER – Emma Duckett
ASSISTANT STAGE MANAGER – Alice Jenkins
LIGHTING DESIGNER – Cassie Mitchell
SOUND DESIGNER & OPERATOR – Laura Merryweather
LIGHTING OPERATOR – Casimira Hayward-Peel

Darkness.

The sound of a strong wind blowing.

Out of the black, an eerie whistling…

VOICE: *(Whistling to this tune.)*
  My bonny lies over the ocean
  My bonny lies over the sea
  My bonny lies over the ocean
  Oh bring back my bonny to – …

  The whistling trails off.

  Lights come up on BARBARA, who blinks groggily against the light.

BARBARA: Harold? Is that you?

  HAROLD enters, brushing dirt from his trousers, and carrying an elegant, ancient vase.

  Do you know what time it is?

HAROLD: Have a look at this, Barb. Gorgeous, isn't it?

  She looks at the vase with a practiced eye.

BARBARA: Oh my. That really is something.

HAROLD: The pottery always survives! The things I'm seeing here, you wouldn't believe it.

  He notices her sleepiness.

  Sorry, did I wake you?

BARBARA: It's alright. I'm glad you came.

HAROLD: There must be hundreds, thousands of artifacts like this. Some going all the way back to the second or third

11

dynasty, the best examples I've ever seen. It's the find of our careers.

BARBARA: Of *your* career.

I miss you.

HAROLD: Bad luck, no way around it.

BARBARA: I thought maybe you weren't coming to see me anymore.

HAROLD: Why would you think that?

BARBARA: It's been so long.

HAROLD: Has it? Time… doesn't feel the same to me anymore.

BARBARA: How does it feel?

HAROLD: Before, it always felt like a place. A set of coordinates to map things onto. Now it feels… alive.

BARBARA: Why do you keep showing up here like this?

HAROLD: Aren't you happy to see me?

BARBARA: How am I supposed to get on with my life when you keep coming round?

HAROLD: Do you want to get on with your life?

BARBARA: I'm trying to be practical.

HAROLD: You know that was never my strong suit.

BARBARA: I woke up the other morning, and I realised I couldn't remember whether you liked your Weetabix hot or cold. I'm forgetting you.

HAROLD: Just the little things.

BARBARA: But it's the little things I want to keep the most.

HAROLD: A man's life is not defined by his breakfast cereal preferences.

BARBARA: I'm still not ready to let you go.

HAROLD: You don't have to, darling. You know how it works. It's like one of our digs. The past never really goes away. It just gets buried a little deeper. If you want to find me, all you have to do is dig.

Suddenly, a loud beeping interrupts their conversation.

Uh oh. Time to go.

BARBARA: Not yet.

HAROLD: Stay strong, keep the faith.

BARBARA: Harold –

HAROLD: I love you.

HAROLD vanishes.

BARBARA wakes up. She is alone.

We discover that the beeping is coming from alarm clock.

BARBARA lashes out at the alarm, switching it off with a bit more force than necessary.

BARBARA: Stupid alarm.

BARBARA gets out of bed, wrapping her arms around herself.

I forgot to ask him where to find the note!

She looks around helplessly, then recalls what he said.

All you have to do is dig.

She has an idea.

BARBARA goes to the bookshelf. She takes a book off her shelf – it is old, with library bindings – and opens it.

BARBARA takes out the paper, very carefully.

She reads:

(Reading.) 'For Barbara –
Oh, my love
My precious rose
My life began the day we met
And every day is better yet.
Oh, the stories we will tell.'

BARBARA closes her eyes. Her face scrunches to keep from crying. She breathes. Her face relaxes. She smiles.

DIG #1

EVE, CATHERINE and the team are fieldwalking. They form an evenly-spaced line and walk together across the playing space. They sweep for surface artifacts, picking up items as they go.

As they pass, CATHERINE picks up BARBARA's note and studies it.

As the team disperses, CATHERINE catches EVE.

CATHERINE: Eve, can I have a word?

EVE: Of course.

CATHERINE: I think it's a bad idea.

EVE: What is?

CATHERINE: Excavating.

EVE: But the team has already started –

CATHERINE: I know.

EVE: Really, are we going to go through all of this again?

CATHERINE: You've seen what we can accomplish through a surface-based survey. There's plenty of interesting material.

EVE: Catherine –

CATHERINE: There's no need to dig.

EVE: It's all small objects, inconsequential things.

CATHERINE: That's not true. Look what I found.

CATHERINE pulls out the note she took from BARBARA and hands it to EVE.

CATHERINE: Read it.

EVE: *(Reading, unimpressed.)* 'Oh my love, my precious rose –'

CATHERINE: You see?

EVE: Well, it's not exactly fine literature, is it?

CATHERINE: But you can't say it doesn't have emotional importance. These are rich finds, whatever you may think.

EVE: I didn't say they weren't. But they don't give us enough context about time or place. Or feeling.

CATHERINE: We can't excavate the site without changing it in some way, damaging it. I don't think we can take the risk.

EVE: I disagree.

CATHERINE: It's one thing at the top layers, with the more recent material. But what about when we get deeper? The earlier memories may be much more fragile.

EVE: Or they may have survived beautifully.

CATHERINE: Once we've started digging, we can't go backwards. We can't undo it. It's best to just leave this site undisturbed, and focus on what's already available to us.

EVE: Which is…? Little notes, odd bits of metal, fragments of pottery?

CATHERINE: Which should be enough. The other artifacts are better off left where they're safe and protected.

EVE: Catherine, it's not that I'm not listening. I hear you. I'm taking your concerns seriously. We're going to proceed as carefully as we can.

CATHERINE: What if we harm the memories? What if we harm the subject?

EVE: It's for her sake that we're here. And I ask you, what good are these memories doing buried where no one can see them or access them?

CATHERINE: But don't you think maybe they're buried and sealed off for a reason?

EVE: Yes. And it's our job to work out what it is.

CATHERINE: Eve –

EVE: Are you in charge of this team, or am I?

CATHERINE: We have a responsibility.

EVE: Yes, we do. And that responsibility is to dig.

A small pause.

CATHERINE: Fine.

EVE: I know that's not what you wanted to hear.

CATHERINE: No. It isn't.

EVE: If you don't want to participate in the excavation, I'll understand.

CATHERINE: I want to stay.

EVE: Are you sure?

CATHERINE nods.

EVE: I'm glad. I couldn't do it without you, you know.

EVE and CATHERINE move over to where the other members of the team are working: EMILY, JOHN, JOANNA, and MARY.

EVE: How are you managing?

JOANNA: Not very well.

MARY: Not very well at all!

EVE: What's the problem?

JOHN: *(To EVE.)* The biggest problem is these two and their moaning.

(To JOANNA and MARY.) If you didn't want to work hard, you shouldn't have signed up to volunteer on an archaeological dig.

JOANNA: We weren't moaning!

JOHN: I mean, really, that's just common sense.

MARY: We're working just as hard as you.

JOHN: Sure. Working with your mouths.

EMILY: *(Scolding.)* John…

JOHN: I just want to be left to dig in peace.

EMILY: *(To JOANNA and MARY.)* Don't mind him. He'll be all sunshine and rainbows after we break through.

17

JOHN: *(To EMILY.)* I wouldn't count on it.

JOANNA and MARY slink back to their stations to continue working.

CATHERINE: Break through what?

JOHN: You can see here.

He shows them where, clearing dirt away from the ground.

JOHN: We just began to dig, and we hit some kind of wall. The area is completely bricked off.

EVE: I wasn't expecting that.

CATHERINE: I was.

JOHN: We're getting through, but it's slow going, because we don't want to damage anything underneath. Obviously.

EVE: How close are you?

JOHN: Close.

Without ceremony, JOHN gets back to work.

EVE: Right.

EMILY: The character of the soil in this area is quite interesting. Look at these samples.

She shows them the soil samples she has collected.

EMILY: Near the surface, it's light-coloured, loose, dry. But then it changed before we even reached the bricks. It's dark, tough, difficult to get through.

EVE: Like clay.

EMILY: Yes. It's almost like another layer sealing up the site. Luckily we've got John. He's got an eye for finding the best way to get through.

CATHERINE: Not to mention that dazzling sense of humour.

From where he is working, JOHN lets out a spontaneous shout.

JOHN: Ha!

EVE: What's that?

JOHN: Told you I was close.

CATHERINE, EVE, and EMILY are joined by MARY and JOANNA, looking at where John has broken through.

JOHN: Just a small gap, but we're finally underneath.

EVE moves in closer to inspect.

EVE: Catherine –

CATHERINE: I'm on it.

CATHERINE snaps photos.

EVE: It's a good thing we were careful. Look at this.

She takes out a china teacup.

EVE: Right there below the surface.

EMILY: Beautiful.

MARY: It's a bit dirty.

CATHERINE: *(With a suppressed smile.)* Yes, that does tend to happen.

EVE: There's another one.

She extracts another.

JOHN: In good condition.

EVE: Only a small chip on this one.

CATHERINE photographs the cup.

EVE: Catherine, will you make sure these get logged?

CATHERINE: Of course.

EVE: And John, let's see what we can do to open up this area and see what else we can find.

JOHN: Roger that.

TEACUPS

FLORENCE and BARBARA in BARBARA's home.

We have moved back to 2011.

It is an absolute wreck, with rubbish everywhere.

BARBARA is strangely over-animated; FLORENCE watches her friend with concern.

BARBARA: They haven't found the plane yet, that's the thing. When they tell me they've found something, then I'll worry.

FLORENCE: Shouldn't someone know something by now?

BARBARA: Well the Egyptian authorities haven't been able to search properly, you know, with all the... instability.

FLORENCE: Of course.

BARBARA: I haven't even offered you something to drink. Shame on me.

FLORENCE: Not to worry.

BARBARA: Tea?

FLORENCE: That would be lovely.

BARBARA: I'll put the kettle on.

BARBARA disappears to the kitchen.

BARBARA: *(Off.)* And I know I've got the nice teacups
somewhere…

FLORENCE: Anything is fine.

BARBARA returns.

BARBARA: They should be – found them!

*BARBARA takes the cups from the team on the dig – without
acknowledging their presence – and gives a cup to FLORENCE.*

Oh no, I'll take the one with the chip.

BARBARA swaps the cups.

*FLORENCE delicately tries to broach a more difficult subject with
BARBARA.*

FLORENCE: How are you managing?

BARBARA: I'm fine.

FLORENCE: *(Delicately.)* It must be different without Harold.

BARBARA: I think that's the kettle.

BARBARA flees into the kitchen.

*While she is gone, FLORENCE has a chance to take in her
surroundings. She peeks into a carrier bag filled with scraps of paper.*

FLORENCE: *(To herself, worried.)* It's an absolute tip.

BARBARA: *(Off, calling in to FLORENCE.)* Would you like any
biscuits?

FLORENCE: I'm alright, thanks.

*FLORENCE hurriedly wipes out her cup with the sleeve of her top,
making sure BARBARA doesn't see.*

BARBARA re-enters with the teapot.

BARBARA: Good thing you said 'no' to the biscuits. As it turns out, I haven't any left.

BARBARA pours the tea.

FLORENCE: So you've been busy, then?

BARBARA: *(Vague.)* Oh, you know…

FLORENCE: The house looks… different.

BARBARA: I didn't think you'd be the type to criticise.

FLORENCE: *(Genuine.)* Barbara, I'm not.

BARBARA: I know it's a bit of a mess. I'm sorry you're seeing it like this.

FLORENCE: Do you need help? Because I'd be happy to –

BARBARA: No, no, I couldn't trouble you with that.

FLORENCE: If you'd like we could take just fifteen minutes and clear a bit of the rubbish out. This for example –

FLORENCE reaches for the carrier bag.

Do you really need this?

BARBARA: Don't touch that!

FLORENCE: It's just a bag of old papers.

BARBARA takes the bag, puts it out of FLORENCE's reach.

BARBARA: It's not.

FLORENCE goes to another bag, this one filled with newspaper clippings.

FLORENCE: Or this? How many old newspapers do you really need?

BARBARA doesn't know how to respond.

I don't mean to meddle, but this isn't good for you, love. It's starting to look like a scene from one of those hoarders' programmes.

BARBARA: I admit it's got away from me a bit –

FLORENCE: Barbara, it isn't hygienic. Why do you have all this stuff lying around?

BARBARA: I want it to be exactly like Harold left it.

FLORENCE: *(Skeptical.)* He left it like this?

BARBARA: It has to be the same when he comes back.

FLORENCE doesn't know what to say to this.

He *is* coming back.

When they tell me they've found the plane –

FLORENCE: I know. You said. That's when you'll worry.

BARBARA: That's right.

FLORENCE: And what in heaven's name are you going to do with yourself in the meantime?

BARBARA: He left something for me, Florence.

FLORENCE: Like what? A message?

BARBARA: Harold always left me these little notes – hidden, so I'd find them at the oddest moments. He'd put them in the strangest places – taped to the underside of a can of beans in the cupboard, folded inside a pair of my socks, buried in the sugar bowl. It was a bit of a game with him.

FLORENCE: I remember.

BARBARA: He left me a note before he left, but I haven't found it yet, and I'm so afraid that I'll throw it out by accident.

FLORENCE: *(Sympathetic.)* But Barbara, how can you ever expect to find it in this?

FLORENCE gestures to the mess in her home.

The phone rings. BARBARA looks away.

Are you going to get that?

BARBARA: I stopped answering a couple of weeks ago. Probably another nosy reporter looking for a comment. Checking to see if I've cracked up yet.

Florence grows uncomfortable with the repeated ringing.

FLORENCE: Should I –?

BARBARA gestures – be my guest.

FLORENCE answers the phone.

(On phone.) Hello?

…

No, this is Florence Holloway. I'm her friend. I'm afraid she can't come to the phone right now –

…

The voice on the other end of the line says something that causes FLORENCE's demeanor to change.

(On the phone.) Just a moment.

She holds the phone away and covers the receiver.

(To BARBARA.) I think you should take this.

BARBARA: Why? Who is it?

FLORENCE holds out the phone and waits. BARBARA – uneasily – takes the phone.

(On the phone.) Hello?

...

Yes, I'm his wife.

...

(Her face changes.)
You found the plane?
I see. Yes, I see.

...

Let me just, um, get a pen.
Just a moment.

BARBARA lowers the phone. She does not go in search of a pen. She does not do anything. She holds the receiver against her chest.

FLORENCE comes over and wraps her arms around BARBARA.

FLORENCE: Shhhh. Breathe. Just breathe.

DIG #2

EVE: How are you getting on?

CATHERINE: Cataloging this section has been a nightmare.

EVE: Really, why?

CATHERINE: I don't know a nicer way to say it. There's loads of stuff, but it's not in good condition. It's mostly junk.

EVE begins to examine the items CATHERINE has unearthed, which includes the bags from the previous scene.

EVE: Like what?

CATHERINE: A range of organic material, which has decayed as you might expect, but then loads of strange stuff as well. Jars full of hundreds of rubber bands, men's clothing that hasn't been washed, old boxes...

EVE: Oh my.

CATHERINE: I would think it was a rubbish dump if it weren't for the fact that the items were so carefully wrapped up and sorted. At least the newspapers have been useful for dating this section.

EVE: Where are those?

CATHERINE: It's this bag here.

CATHERINE picks up the bag filled with newspaper clippings.

EVE: Have you already gone through them?

CATHERINE: Mmm. The oldest dates from January 2011, and there are newer ones from as recently as late 2013.

They sort through the papers. EVE spots one that catches her eye. She reads aloud.

EVE: *(Reading.)* 'Protests erupt in Egypt...'

CATHERINE: There's another pile with Joanna and Mary. I thought sorting them might be a good task for them.

EVE: Give John a break?

CATHERINE: Exactly.

EVE: The papers will be an enormous help in dating when the teacups were deposited. Were you thinking late 2013?

CATHERINE: Or even as recently as 2014.

EVE: Possible, certainly.

EVE begins to construct the timeline.

EVE: Where are the photo printouts?

CATHERINE: Here.

CATHERINE gets out the photos.

They write dates on the timeline: 'Jan 2011', 'April 2013'.

CATHERINE: So we'll put the cups and the rubbish in this period.

CATHERINE sticks a polaroid (or digital printout) of the teacups next to 'April 2013'.

EVE: Now, about the love note we found on the surface –

JOHN: Ladies, I've got something else over here you might be interested in.

EVE: We'll be right over.

CATHERINE and EVE hurriedly finish their conversation.

CATHERINE: The note definitely came later.

EVE writes '2014?' on the board. CATHERINE posts the photo of the note next to it.

The women go to where JOHN is working.

He extracts a flower vase from the ground.

ROGER appears, and takes the vase out of JOHN's hands.

FLOWER VASE

BARBARA's home.

BARBARA answers the door. It's ROGER.

He holds the vase. It is now filled with flowers.

He looks incredibly uncomfortable – nervous, miserable, and scared.

BARBARA: Roger?

ROGER: Hello.

BARBARA: Is everything alright?

ROGER: Yes. Sorry. I hope you don't mind me stopping by –

BARBARA: Not at all.

ROGER: I mean, we could have spoken at the University, but I thought it might be easier here.

BARBARA: Yes?

ROGER: I was so sure. I was so sure everything was going to be fine.

BARBARA: What happened?

ROGER: We know for certain that the plane took off. But it doesn't look like it ever landed. I'm sorry, I'm not used to delivering news like this.

BARBARA: I don't understand.

ROGER: They got a charter flight from the site. That's been confirmed. You know, one of those tiny little planes –

BARBARA: Yes, I know –

ROGER: The plane crashed.

It takes BARBARA a moment to find her voice.

BARBARA: Are you sure?

ROGER: We're ninety percent certain.

BARBARA: Is Harold alive? And his team...

ROGER: We haven't heard from any of them. And the region isn't stable enough to mount a proper search.

BARBARA: So he could still be alive.

ROGER: Anything's possible.

BARBARA nods.

BARBARA: I think I'd like to be alone.

ROGER: Of course. Of course.

He starts to leave, with a worried glance at BARBARA.

A few steps away, he realises he is still holding the flowers. He turns back.

These are for you.

BARBARA accepts the vase.

BARBARA: Thank you.

ROGER: I'm sorry.

ROGER departs, as a man pursued.

DIG #3

The memory site team take the vase from BARBARA's hands, moving it to the artifact table.

CATHERINE finds JOHN.

CATHERINE: Taking a break?

JOHN: Yeah. Letting the girls get on with it for a while.

CATHERINE: 'The girls?'

JOHN: You know, Tweedledum and Tweedledee.

CATHERINE: Are they really that bad?

JOHN: I just don't see why we need to bring a load of volunteers in. Though I don't know if you can even call them volunteers if they're paying to spend their holidays tagging along.

CATHERINE: You know it helps the work go faster. And you shouldn't call them 'girls', John.

JOHN: Wasn't my idea, they came up with that nickname themselves.

CATHERINE: Really?

JOHN: Yeah. They got tired of being "number one" and "number two."

CATHERINE: I can't imagine why.

JOHN softens a bit.

JOHN: I'm not being that rough on them. They're having the time of their lives.

CATHERINE: I know.

JOHN: *(Snapping back to his usual, wry self.)* If only I could say the same for me.

CATHERINE: Can I ask you a question? What do you think of this project?

JOHN: Not my job to think. That's what you lot are here for.

CATHERINE: John, I'm worried about this site. I'm worried about what will happen when we get too deep.

JOHN: Did you talk to Eve?

CATHERINE: Yes.

JOHN: Is she worried?

CATHERINE: No.

JOHN: Then I reckon it's fine.

CATHERINE: But don't you have a funny feeling about this one?

JOHN: That rubbish section was a bit odd, but we're through that now.

CATHERINE: I mean the site as a whole.

JOHN: It's an unusual shape, strange kind of layering in places, but I'm sure it'll make more sense when we get a bit lower.

CATHERINE: Maybe.

JOHN: Why are you so worried? What do you think is going to happen?

CATHERINE: Honestly? I have no idea.

There is a cry from the area where MARY and JOANNA are working, with EVE keeping an eye on things.

JOANNA: Oh, would you look at that?

MARY: Incredible!

JOHN hurries over, followed by CATHERINE.

JOHN: What's happening over here?

EVE: John, it looks like your team has made quite the find.

JOANNA: Look.

She pulls out a casserole dish.

JOHN: Not bad.

MARY: There's more.

MARY and JOANNA keep taking out casserole dishes, until there are four lined up in a row.

CATHERINE: Four casserole dishes? That seems like a lot.

MARY: Not at all. My sister-in-law has five.

MARY gets a strange look from the others.

MARY: Well, she does!

CASSEROLES

BARBARA is searching through her house, looking for HAROLD's note.

BARBARA: It's got to be here. It's got to be here somewhere.

The doorbell rings. BARBARA opens the door. JOYCE and SHARON are there holding casserole dishes.

SHARON: Oh, Barbara!

SHARON shoves her casserole dish at JOYCE and throws her arms around BARBARA.

How are you holding up?

BARBARA: I'm fine.

SHARON: Now, don't give me that.

BARBARA: Really, I'm fine. You didn't have to –

SHARON: Of course we did!

(To JOYCE.) Joyce, what are you doing? Get those in the fridge!

The women enter BARBARA's home.

JOYCE takes the dishes to the fridge.

Are we the first, then?

BARBARA: The first what?

SHARON: I called around to organise the rest of the girls from choir.

BARBARA: To do what?

The doorbell rings again.

SHARON: *(To BARBARA.)* Do you want to get that?

BARBARA goes to the door. It's ANNE, holding a dish.

BARBARA: Anne?

ANNE: Barbara, how are you?

BARBARA: I'm fine.

SHARON: Joyce, we've got another one for the fridge.

JOYCE comes and takes ANNE's dish.

ANNE: *(To JOYCE.)* Thank you.

JOYCE smiles weakly in return, and carries the plate into the kitchen.

BARBARA: *(To SHARON.)* How many people did you call?

SHARON: Just the alto section.

The doorbell rings again. It's JULIE (plus casserole). She goes straight to BARBARA.

JULIE: Oh, Barbara, love –

BARBARA: I'm fine thanks.

SHARON: *(To JULIE.)* You can give that to Joyce.

BARBARA: What is going on!?

Everyone is a bit stunned.

SHARON: Well, it's been all over the news, hasn't it? About the violence in… what's it called. That place in Egypt, you know.

BARBARA: So…?

SHARON: Well, that's where Harold is. Was. Right? That's where his dig –

BARBARA: Yes.

SHARON: They said his name and everything. It's like you were famous.

JULIE: We simply thought you might want a little support. Given… everything.

BARBARA: But why are you stuffing my refrigerator full of food?

She suddenly realises what's really going on.

You think he's dead. Don't you?

JULIE: Barbara –

BARBARA: That's why you've all come.

(To SHARON.) That's why you've got them all over.

(To the group.) You all think he's dead.

JULIE: Well –

ANNE: I don't. I think he's alive and well and stubborn as ever. All I know is, I wouldn't like to be spending my time in the kitchen while I'm busy worrying about someone.

BARBARA: But if you think he's fine, why should I be worrying?

SHARON: Because it's a bloody revolution, of course you're worried. You don't have to pretend with us, Barbara.

BARBARA: I'm not pretending anything. He's fine. I know it. I know it in my heart.

JULIE: I'm sure he is.

BARBARA: That's what Roger said: it's too soon to tell.

ANNE: Who's Roger?

BARBARA: He's one of our colleagues at the University. He's coordinating the... response. I went in to speak with him yesterday.

SHARON: What did he say?

BARBARA: The team got out. They arranged a charter flight to evacuate before the site was attacked.

ANNE: That's wonderful.

JULIE: Oh, Barbara, I'm so relieved.

SHARON: Well, obviously. We all are.

JULIE: How did Harold sound when you spoke to him?

BARBARA: Well, I haven't spoken to him yet.

ANNE: Oh. Did Roger speak with him?

BARBARA: No, they're going from reports they've had from their colleagues in Egypt.

ANNE: Oh, right.

SHARON: Has anyone spoken to him?

BARBARA: They'd lost touch –

SHARON: But that was days ago. Anything could have happened.

ANNE: Sharon!

SHARON: Well it could. Don't you want some answers?

BARBARA: Do you honestly think I haven't been trying to get them?

SHARON: Of course not, that's not what I meant.

BARBARA exits to the kitchen.

ANNE: Honestly, Sharon.

SHARON: What?

ANNE: Did you see how upset you made her?

SHARON: That's not my fault. It's just the facts, isn't it? Do you think he's coming back?

ANNE: That isn't the point.

SHARON: It would be a miracle, that's what I said – didn't I, Joyce – an absolute miracle.

ANNE: Yes, and sometimes miracles happen.

SHARON: Yeah, on telly programmes.

JULIE: I think we've made her feel worse.

ANNE: *(To SHARON.)* You should apologise.

SHARON: For what? I spent half an hour making that casserole. Out of the goodness of my own heart.

JULIE: We know, Sharon.

SHARON: I mean, really. Apologise?

ANNE: Can you at least try to be a bit more sensitive?

SHARON: Fine, have it your way! I won't say anything at all.

ANNE: Sharon…

BARBARA re-enters.

BARBARA: Sorry. I needed to check something in the kitchen.

ANNE: It's fine.

JULIE: Please. Don't you worry about us.

BARBARA: It's just… I've spent my whole life worried about him being one place or another – or leaving him to worry about me. It's a fact of life in this line of work. Harold and

I have always said that no news is good news. I'll worry when I have something to worry about.

ANNE: Hear, hear.

JULIE: Of course, Barbara.

BARBARA: *(To SHARON, with warmth.)* Sharon?

SHARON: Yes?

BARBARA: I know you meant it kindly. Coming with the food and everything.

SHARON: I'm just trying to be supportive.

BARBARA: Of course you are.

SHARON: Look after my fellow woman and all that.

JULIE: Yes, Sharon.

SHARON: *(With a pointed look at ANNE.)* And I really don't appreciate people telling me I'm not being sensitive.

BARBARA: I know.

It's fine. Because they would have told me. They would have told me if...

BARBARA loses her words.

The others stare on, uncomfortably.

JOYCE comes over to BARBARA, and gives her a hug.

This gesture means more than any words could. BARBARA's physicality softens a bit.

Thank you, Joyce.

JOYCE: My pleasure.

BARBARA: So... Four casseroles. Who's hungry?

DIG #4

EVE surveys the change in atmosphere in the site.

EVE: Look at this area. This is different.

JOANNA: What does it mean?

CATHERINE: It looks like we're seeing artifacts that originated from an entirely different location.

EVE: From the same subject's source memories, though. The same person.

JOANNA: Is that good?

EVE: It's excellent news. It means we're getting an even better picture of the subject's activity.

CATHERINE: But we're also disturbing artifacts over an even wider span than you originally projected.

JOHN notices a pen lying on the site. He picks it up and examines it.

JOHN: Nice pen.

JOANNA: So what is the new location?

EVE: *(To JOANNA, drawing her out.)* What do you think?

JOHN: *(Impatient, wanting to get on with things.)* Come on, really?

The others ignore him.

JOANNA: I don't know. That metal looks like it might be a filing cabinet.

EVE: Good. And this?

JOANNA: It doesn't look like much of anything.

EVE: Can you tell what it's made out of?

JOANNA: Wood?

EVE: Very good. Are there any other clues.

JOANNA: Well, it's the right size for…do you think it's a desk?

EVE: Very good.

JOHN: Desk, filing cabinets – it's an office, alright?

EVE sighs with annoyance at JOHN.

EVE: Thanks, John. Catherine, bag that pen, will you?

CATHERINE takes the pen away from JOHN.

PEN

ROGER's office. ROGER and BARBARA.

ROGER: Really, Barbara, I'm doing all I can. This is mountains out of molehills. He'll be fine.

BARBARA: Shouldn't we know more?

ROGER: We're ninety percent sure he and the others got out before the bombs hit.

BARBARA: But what about that other ten percent?

ROGER: I've been in touch with people in the government about this, but there's rather a lot going on at the moment.

BARBARA: But if he got out, why haven't I heard from him?

ROGER: I don't know. Everything indicates that they took a charter flight three days ago –

BARBARA smiles.

Why are you smiling?

BARBARA: That's the day after I spoke to him. He actually listened. I'm just surprised, that's all.

ROGER: So who knows – they may have had to land and keep quiet for a little while.

BARBARA: He should never have gone back there.

ROGER: Look, I'm fairly certain that everything is going to be fine. This isn't the first time you two have been in a scrape.

BARBARA: Yes. But I'm not used to being the one left behind. I really think we should at least consider that I go –

ROGER: You really want to run off to Egypt looking for him?

BARBARA: Because I speak the language, I know people –

ROGER: Right. And how good is Harold's Arabic?

BARBARA: Well, he's fluent, but –

ROGER: And does he know people there?

BARBARA: You know Harold, he could make friends with a log.

ROGER: So if by some bad luck he has wound up in a mess, it's not language skills or lack of connections that are going to be the issue, are they?

BARBARA: I suppose it's not much of a plan.

ROGER: No, it isn't. And I don't think he'd thank me for sending you off after him. Do you?

BARBARA: Probably not.

ROGER: So for now the best thing we can do is wait.

BARBARA: I was never very good at being patient.

ROGER: Mmmm. I've noticed.

DIG #5

EVE: Right, so we've got –

CATHERINE posts the relevant photos as EVE speaks, putting them in reverse chronological order, moving to the left.

Flower vase...

Casserole dishes...

CATHERINE: And the pen.

CATHERINE pins the photo to the chart.

EVE: Things seem to be coming together.

EMILY comes over, carrying detailed drawings.

EMILY: And I have even better news for you.

EVE: What?

EMILY: We're beginning to get a sense of the structure of the underlying landscape. These are the latest diagrams we've made of the site.

CATHERINE takes the diagrams and has a look.

EVE: Let me see.

CATHERINE passes the drawings to EVE.

EVE: Quite a steep slope there.

JOHN: Are those the drawings?

EVE: Yes.

JOHN: Can I have a look?

EVE hands the drawings to JOHN.

EVE: Wider and deeper than any of us had predicted.

JOHN: It looks like a pit. A giant hole. Filled in and closed off.

CATHERINE: Or a bomb crater.

JOHN: Yeah, exactly.

EVE: Given what we know about the subject, that sounds about right.

TELEVISION

The phone rings. BARBARA answers.

BARBARA: Hello?

FLORENCE: Barbara, it's Florence.

BARBARA: How are you, Florence?

FLORENCE: Turn on the news.

BARBARA: What?

FLORENCE: Have you seen the news?

BARBARA: No.

FLORENCE: Turn it on.

Still holding the phone, BARBARA goes to her television and turns on the news.

NEWSREADER: … immeasurable destruction to history. Following in the wake of increased activity from rebel forces in Egypt, the government has stepped in with a military response. Bombers have hit a number of suspected rebel camps, however an unexpected casualty has been the site of –

BARBARA: Oh my God.

NEWSREADER: Witnesses report that the site was hit in the early hours of the morning. The extent of the damage is not yet known, nor is the fate of the team of archaeologists working on the site, but –

FLORENCE: I'm coming over now.

FLORENCE hangs up. BARBARA continues watching the news, in a daze.

NEWSREADER: – priceless loss of artifacts from one of the most famous tombs in Egypt, which was listed as a UNESCO World Heritage site. Of equal concern is the fate of the archaeologists. Reportedly, there were six Britons on the team working there –

BARBARA watches, dry-eyed, in shock.

BARBARA: *(Quietly, to herself.)* You stupid, stupid man.

DIG #6

EVE pins a photo of the television onto the timeline.

CATHERINE approaches with JOHN, carrying a soil sample.

CATHERINE: Eve, have you seen this?

EVE: What?

CATHERINE: Look at this. The soil is completely different.

EVE examines the sample.

EVE: Not even soil. Sand.

CATHERINE: I don't understand it.

JOHN: The site must have been contaminated.

EVE: But how?

CATHERINE: Who knows?

EVE: But we would have seen items that were disturbed or damaged if there had been interference at the site. There hasn't been anything like that.

JOHN: Except lots and lots of sand.

CATHERINE: There's even more of it over there.

JOHN: I've never seen anything like it.

EVE: We shouldn't get ahead of ourselves. We won't know anything until we analyse it. It could just mean she was experimenting in the garden.

CATHERINE: Do you think that's it?

EVE: No. What do you reckon?

CATHERINE: You remember the book. The papers about Cairo. I think it's Egyptian.

EVE examines the sand.

EVE: Could be.

CATHERINE: I don't think it's a coincidence. Strange as it seems.

EVE: Has Emily seen this?

CATHERINE: She's looking at it now.

EVE: Good.

PHONE CALL

BARBARA is on the phone with HAROLD.

HAROLD: Don't be ridiculous, it's perfectly safe.

BARBARA: Don't patronise me, Harold, I know as well as you do that if the conflict gets worse you could end up right in the thick of it.

HAROLD: And if that happens, who is going to look after the site?

BARBARA: Harold –

HAROLD: This is our life's work, Barbara. After fifty years, you want me simply to walk away from all we've done?

BARBARA: I want you to be sensible.

HAROLD: The thing to do is just put your head down and wait it out. If you were here and you could see it for yourself, you'd say exactly the same thing.

BARBARA: But I'm not there, am I?

HAROLD: You could have come –

BARBARA: I couldn't have, and don't lie by saying otherwise. I would have slowed down the whole team, it wouldn't have been safe.

HAROLD: Maybe if you'd had the replacement surgery –

BARBARA: I don't want to argue about my knees!

HAROLD: Well you clearly want to bicker about something.

BARBARA: I want you to come home.

HAROLD: Barbara, I can't.

BARBARA: Is it more important than me? The site, the dig, all that. Is it more important to you than I am?

HAROLD: That's a ridiculous question.

BARBARA: Is it?

HAROLD: Of course it's not, but you shouldn't make me choose!

BARBARA: I'm not making you choose, I'm trying to keep you safe.

HAROLD: I'm not ready to retire and sit at home like you.

BARBARA: I'm not asking you to.

HAROLD: Oh, right.

BARBARA: Even if you don't care about yourself, what about your team? They have families, futures. You need to get them out of there.

HAROLD: Everyone who's chosen to stay wants to be here.

BARBARA: Yes, and I want to go to the moon, but that doesn't mean it's a good idea.

HAROLD: I've had enough of this.

BARBARA: Tell me about it.

HAROLD: I've been doing this work for fifty years, and if you think I don't have the sense to know when it's time to get out, you don't know anything.

BARBARA: Fine! And if something happens to you, on your head be it, you stubborn old ass!

HAROLD: Goodbye.

BARBARA: Goodbye.

BARBARA and HAROLD both hang up the phone.

You stupid, stupid man.

DIG #7

EVE and CATHERINE are taking a tea break.

EVE: Any word yet on the sand?

CATHERINE: Not yet.

Do you ever think about what it's like?

EVE: What what's like?

CATHERINE: Being the subject.

EVE: Sometimes.

CATHERINE: I think about it. I think about it a lot.

EVE: That doesn't surprise me.

CATHERINE: Sometimes I have dreams about it. Feeling memories awaken that you thought you'd forgotten. Maybe that you wanted to forget.

EVE: Whether you remember or whether you forget, it doesn't change the fact that the moment existed. It doesn't change the fact that, in one way or another, an artifact is still there.

CATHERINE: I'm beginning to see why you thought it was important to excavate this subject. In spite of the dangers.

EVE: Really?

CATHERINE: She needs these memories, doesn't she?

EVE: If she didn't, we wouldn't be here.

CATHERINE drinks her tea.

CATHERINE: The girls certainly do know how to make a cup of tea, don't they?

EVE: Even John has to give them that.

WHISPERS

The site of HAROLD's archaeological dig.

HAROLD enters, with his team in tow, then steps off the side to consult with one of them about the dig.

MAGGIE and LOU speak privately.

MAGGIE: Harold might not have heard about the rumours yet.

LOU: You should say something.

MAGGIE: I don't want to step on his toes.

LOU: This isn't anything to be messed around with. If you don't talk to him, I will.

MAGGIE: Fine.

MAGGIE approaches HAROLD.

Harold, do you have a minute?

HAROLD: Of course. What's going on, Maggie?

MAGGIE: Well, it's just that Lou and I were talking to Ahmed...

LOU: He's been hearing some troubling things. About what's been happening in the area.

MAGGIE: He thinks that maybe we should consider...

MAGGIE looks to LOU for help.

LOU: He's worried that it isn't safe here anymore. For any of us.

HAROLD: I see. And what do you think?

MAGGIE: I don't know. Ahmed isn't the type to exaggerate. He knows what he's talking about.

HAROLD: What do you think, Lou?

LOU: Seems alright to me, but better to be safe.

HAROLD: Right.

LOU: Harold, we know you don't want to hear it.

MAGGIE: We're not trying to make trouble.

LOU: But we thought you ought to know.

HAROLD: I see. Could you gather the group? Call over the others? I'd like to make an announcement.

LOU: Sure.

MAGGIE and LOU bring over FRANK and his team and HELEN and her team.

HAROLD takes a moment to collect his thoughts, while the group gathers.

HAROLD: Hello everyone – sorry for stopping your work. I've just had a chat with Maggie and Lou here about some reports of instability in the area. I'm sure this news must have reached some of you as well. Am I right?

There are a few nervous glances between people in the group. HELEN speaks up.

HELEN: I'd heard something.

HAROLD: Well, I wanted to take a moment to say that no one should feel under any pressure to stay if they aren't comfortable. No hard feelings – you're welcome to just pack up and go.

FRANK: What are you going to do?

49

HAROLD: I've been working in this region long enough – and I know it's true for some of you as well – that I think I'm tough enough to weather a few ups and downs.

MAGGIE: I heard that the Foreign Office was making recommendations to evacuate people.

HAROLD: Not in our area. They're being intelligent about it. Strategic. But that doesn't mean you have to stay if you don't feel safe.

FRANK: You didn't answer my question. What are you going to do?

HAROLD: I'm going to wait a few weeks and see how things shake out. Of course if things get worse, we'll evacuate sooner, but I can't imagine stepping away at this stage. Looters would have a field day with this place.

LOU: Harold – I'm not trying to be funny, but you seem awfully relaxed about all this?

HAROLD: *(Playful, over-the-top nonchalant.)* Do I?

He fans himself casually with his hat, drawing a few grins from the crowd, but the mood quickly returns to a serious tone.

MAGGIE: What if something does happen? Do we have any kind of plan?

HAROLD: Of course.

FRANK: Well? What is it?

HAROLD: I've made arrangements for us to fly the team out immediately at the first sign of any real danger.

HELEN: And what about the site?

HAROLD: We'd leave it.

HELEN: And the Egyptian team?

HAROLD: Honestly, Helen, if it comes to that it's out of our hands.

LOU: How will you know when it's time to go?

HAROLD: I'll know.

DIG #8

EMILY approaches EVE and CATHERINE.

EMILY: There you are.

EVE: Do you have an answer about the sand?

EMILY: I do.

EVE: And?

EMILY: Well, it's impossible to say for certain without laboratory analysis –

EVE: But?

EMILY: But from what I can see, it's absolutely consistent with what you would find in Egyptian sites bordering on the Sahara.

CATHERINE and EVE look at each other.

EMILY: You don't seem pleased. Catherine, I thought this Egyptian suggestion was your idea.

CATHERINE: It was. But it also means our site is contaminated.

EMILY: Why do you assume that?

CATHERINE: What other explanation is there?

EVE: If it was earlier in the timeline of events, that would make sense. After all, the subject spent years in Egypt.

CATHERINE: Yes, but she wasn't in Egypt during this time, she was in England. It isn't consistent with the documentary evidence we have for this period. So it could signify hallucinations, or worse: that her memories are... no longer reliable.

EMILY: On the contrary, I think it makes perfect sense.

CATHERINE: How so?

EMILY: Because maybe that's where her heart and mind were at the time. It would be perfectly reasonable for her to have thoughts or memories rooted there. It doesn't mean she's losing her faculties.

CATHERINE: Hmm. It's possible that's true.

(To EVE.) What do you think?

EVE: I suspect that, as usual, Emily is probably right.

CATHERINE: Right. The sand is in.

CATHERINE adds a photo of sand to the timeline, and a soil sample to the table of artifacts.

THEATRE TICKETS

BARBARA searching through her house.

BARBARA: Where in God's name could he have left it? He always was a sneaky one.

She realises she's speaking to herself.

(To herself.) Oh dear.

FLORENCE arrives.

Florence! Oh, I'm glad you're here.

FLORENCE: Now that's a welcome.

BARBARA: You should have heard me. He's gone twenty-four hours and I'm talking to myself already. Give me a few days and I'll be positively climbing the walls.

FLORENCE: Well that's why I'm here to cheer you up! Were you at least talking about something interesting?

BARBARA: No, just looking for something.

FLORENCE: Do you want help?

BARBARA: No, it's... I'll sort it out later.

FLORENCE: I don't mind.

BARBARA: Thanks, Florence, but that's alright. So what is this play we're going to see?

FLORENCE takes out the tickets to have a look.

FLORENCE: Honestly, I've no idea. Some rubbish out on tour.

BARBARA: *(Sarcastic.)* Sounds wonderful.

FLORENCE: But it has that actor, you know, the one with the beard? I know he has a beard. And I think there's a juggler, so that's something.

BARBARA: I like jugglers.

FLORENCE: I know. I'm just so pleased you could take the day off.

BARBARA: *(Evasive.)* Yes, well...

FLORENCE: Barbara?

BARBARA: I'll have more days off for a while.

FLORENCE: Why?

BARBARA: I took a leave of absence from the University.

FLORENCE: Barbara, are you serious? Why would you do that? You love your work. Don't you?

BARBARA: Yes, but it occurred to me that I don't really know what to do with myself when Harold is gone. Or when I'm not working. And I don't want to wake up one morning, alone in a stuffy house and realise I haven't got anything else.

FLORENCE: That's fair enough.

BARBARA: And maybe it's time for us to scale our research back a bit. Harold would never retire completely, but it would be nice to have a bit more time to just enjoy life. Relax a little.

FLORENCE: Well, I wouldn't count on retirement for relaxation. Enjoyment, definitely, but I can tell you, I've never been busier.

BARBARA: Yes, well I wouldn't sign up for ten million meetings and classes and whatnot. Like you do.

FLORENCE: That's a slight exaggeration.

BARBARA: You know what I mean.

FLORENCE: And what would you do?

BARBARA: Honestly, I've no idea. But I'm looking forward to finding out.

ARRIVAL

The site of HAROLD's archaeological dig.

HAROLD strides up, accompanied by his team.

HAROLD: And here we are! God, I've missed Egypt.

FRANK: The heat surprises me every time. You think I'd get used to it.

HAROLD: Give it a few more years.

FRANK: That's what you said to me ten years ago.

HAROLD: God, I've missed this place.

LOU: *(Laughing.)* Look at you! Like a kid in a sweet shop.

HAROLD: Be careful, or I'll start the digging early.

MAGGIE: I've spoken with the local team, and we're all set for tomorrow morning.

HAROLD: That's great. Thanks, Maggie. We can go ahead and start unpacking. Helen, do you want to work with Frank to mark out the area.

HELEN: Sure.

FRANK: Who's cooking tonight?

LOU: Helen drew the short straw, didn't she?

HELEN: Only if you're willing to eat my cooking.

MAGGIE: And risk eating crunchy pasta again? No thank you.

HELEN: It was al dente!

MAGGIE: I'll cook. You lot can do the dishes.

FRANK: Works for me.

HELEN, FRANK, and MAGGIE disperse, busy with their tasks.

LOU: You really love it here, don't you?

HAROLD: It's the only reason I'd pick up and leave Barbara for this long.

LOU: Must be strange coming on your own.

HAROLD: I can't help it. It's in my blood. It feels like home.

DIG #9

CATHERINE is actively working on the dig.

CATHERINE: Finally! It looks like we've just about reached the end of the mysterious sand!

JOHN: Too bad really.

EMILY: Why is that?

JOHN: I like sand. It's easier to dig.

EVE: Well, I for one don't mind that we seem to be back on solid ground.

CATHERINE: There's a big mass down here.

EVE: Can you see what it is?

CATHERINE: Almost. Let me just –

JOHN: I'll give you a hand.

CATHERINE keeps working, aided by JOHN, and the items become visible.

CATHERINE: Well, I wasn't expecting that.

EVE: What have you found now?

CATHERINE pulls out a pair of socks.

CATHERINE: It's an enormous pile of socks.

SOCKS

BARBARA grabs the socks and chases after HAROLD with them.

BARBARA: Did you pack enough socks?

HAROLD: Yes.

BARBARA: You never pack enough socks.

HAROLD: I did this time.

BARBARA: You don't want blisters.

HAROLD: I know, love.

BARBARA: What about your passport? Do you have your passport?

HAROLD: No, I figured it wasn't really a priority – space being tight and all –

BARBARA: You are incorrigible.

HAROLD: I try to be.

BARBARA takes a moment, looking at him.

BARBARA: What am I going to do without you?

HAROLD: Well, there's always scrapbooking…

BARBARA: That's not funny.

HAROLD: Or decoupage?

BARBARA: It feels so strange. Sending you off on an adventure instead of joining you on one.

HAROLD: Well, next time it will be both of us. We'll get your knees all fixed up and –

BARBARA: You don't have to go.

HAROLD: *(Serious.)* Are you really asking me to stay?

BARBARA makes her decision.

She goes and tucks the socks into his bag.

BARBARA: I don't know what you'll do without me there to keep you on schedule. You'll be a month behind within a week.

HAROLD: I'll have Helen and Frank on the case, they've very good.

BARBARA: Yes, they are very good.

HAROLD checks his watch.

HAROLD: I should be going.

HAROLD and BARBARA fold into each other's arms, like they never want to let go.

BARBARA: Take care of yourself.

HAROLD: I will.

BARBARA: Be safe.

HAROLD: I will.

BARBARA: Come back to me soon.

HAROLD: I will. I promise.

BARBARA: I love you.

HAROLD: I love you, too.

HAROLD picks up his shoulder bag.

Oh, and one more thing.

BARBARA: What?

HAROLD: I left you something.

BARBARA: What is it?

HAROLD: Nothing, just a little surprise.

BARBARA: *(Worried.)* Harold…

HAROLD: Don't worry, it's not alive. Nothing that will rot or cause damage or any of that. Just a little something for you to keep an eye out for while I'm away.

BARBARA: Please tell me you stayed out of the kitchen this time.

HAROLD: I think this one will take you a while. You have to let me know when you find it.

BARBARA: Do I get a clue?

HAROLD grins.

HAROLD: I love you.

He gives her a peck on the cheek, and heads out of the door.

She waves as the taxi pulls away.

BARBARA: Goodbye. Goodbye.

BARBARA closes her eyes tightly.

Goodbye.

DIG #10 / SEEING NEW

When BARBARA opens her eyes, she finds herself on the memory site, and discovers that she can now see the site and its team, including EVE and CATHERINE.

BARBARA is wary, confused, and a bit frightened of this change in circumstances.

For the moment, EVE's team continues with their work, unaware of her presence.

JOHN is digging when he makes a surprise find.

JOHN: Whoa. Oh, this is good.

JOANNA: What is it?

JOHN: *(To JOANNA and MARY.)* You're going to love this, girls.

MARY: I can't see.

JOHN: There's a whole pocket here that looks to be from a completely different era. Like we just jumped back fifty years.

EVE: Really?

JOHN: Have a look for yourself.

BARBARA: Hello?

The team stares at BARBARA in shock.

EVE moves forward, extending her hand.

EVE: You must be Barbara.

BARBARA accepts the handshake, still a bit confused.

BARBARA notices that CATHERINE is holding the socks that appeared in the previous scene.

BARBARA: Those are Harold's socks.

CATHERINE: Yes.

BARBARA spots the timeline. She is stunned at what she sees.

BARBARA: Those... That's my...

EVE: It's all yours. All of it.

BARBARA: I didn't know whether any of it would still be here.

BARBARA goes to the sand, runs her fingers through it.

BARBARA: I'm dreaming again, aren't I?

EVE: Does it matter?

CATHERINE: We weren't sure whether you were going to come.

BARBARA: It took me a bit longer than I expected. To be ready. I wanted to dig, I wanted to remember. But I couldn't.

EVE: Not to worry. We've been getting everything ready for you.

BARBARA: Oh, right.

CATHERINE: We don't know if you'll agree with the sorting we've done so far, but it's a start.

BARBARA: Thank you.

EVE: Pleasure. Do you want to have a look?

BARBARA: You mean, now?

EVE: Yes, why not?

BARBARA: Well, um –

JOHN: You're here just in time for the good stuff.

BARBARA: Really?

EVE: *(Delicately.)* Yes, we've set aside the more recent materials –

CATHERINE: There was quite a lot.

EVE: You can look at those later. But we've just uncovered a cache of older artifacts.

BARBARA: From when?

EVE: You can see for yourself.

JOHN extracts an old magazine, and passes it to BARBARA.

BARBARA: Why, this must be from fifty years ago.

EVE: I know why you've been waiting to come here, but you shouldn't be afraid. It's not just painful. There are wonderful things.

CATHERINE: Like the magazine. Do you remember?

EVE and CATHERINE watch BARBARA's face, as the memory of this particular moment comes back to her.

BARBARA: It could almost be from when Florence and I lived together as students…

FLORENCE – now in her twenties – enters and takes the magazine from CATHERINE. She flips it open and begins to read.

BARBARA: Florence was always reading some silly magazine or other.

CATHERINE: She remembers.

Suddenly, BARBARA is again also in her twenties, and walks into the scene –

BOOK

A modest flat. Approximately fifty years earlier than the start of the play. FLORENCE reads the magazine.

BARBARA enters.

FLORENCE: *(Like a cat that's caught a sparrow.)* Oh, hello, Barbara.

BARBARA: Hello yourself. And what are you looking so smug about?

FLORENCE shrugs, casually.

FLORENCE: Nothing. Someone came by to see you.

BARBARA: Who?

FLORENCE: A man. He left something for you.

FLORENCE gestures to a book. It's the same one BARBARA opened to find HAROLD's last note at the beginning of the play.

BARBARA picks it up with growing excitement.

Looks like a real page-turner.

BARBARA: It is. It's all about the techniques the Egyptians used to mummify their Pharaohs –

FLORENCE: Honestly, Barbara, you have the strangest way of getting a boyfriend.

BARBARA: He's not my boyfriend. Not yet.

BARBARA opens the book.

A note falls out.

BARBARA: *(To herself.)* What's this?

Surprised and confused, BARBARA picks it up and opens it. As she reads, she smiles.

FLORENCE: What's it say?

BARBARA: It's private.

FLORENCE: Come on.

BARBARA hesitates, then reads aloud, pleased but still a bit shy.

BARBARA: *(Reading.)* 'For Barbara –
A beautiful girl with a beautiful name
The Pharaohs would say she's one fine dame'

BARBARA and FLORENCE cringe and burst into giggles.

BARBARA is whirled away –

DIG #11

BARBARA is back with CATHERINE and EVE.

BARBARA: That was the first note he ever sent me.

EVE: Yes.

BARBARA: The first. I thought I'd lost it years ago.

EVE: It's been here all along.

BARBARA: How much is here? Is there more?

HAROLD enters, in his twenties.

BARBARA: Harold?

HAROLD is unaware of BARBARA, and cannot hear her. His eyes scan a room we cannot yet see.

BARBARA: He looks just like the day we met. With that horrid jacket. How strange.

EVE: Barbara, do you really think that's a coincidence?

JOHN takes two glasses out of the ground – these are passed to HAROLD.

EVE and CATHERINE guide BARBARA into the next scene.

COCKTAIL GLASSES

A few days before the previous scene in the flat. This is the date of BARBARA and HAROLD's first official meeting.

At a party. There is music. Guests mill about – they talk, and laugh, and dance.

BARBARA stands alone, holding a drink.

HAROLD approaches, holding two drinks. BARBARA is visibly irritated by his presence but doesn't acknowledge him. He sidles up next to her.

HAROLD: You don't like me, do you?

BARBARA rolls her eyes.

BARBARA: Hello.

HAROLD: I knew it. You don't like me.

BARBARA: Don't you have someone else to bother?

HAROLD: No, I picked you. You looked like you were having too much fun over here by yourself. You know, all alone.

BARBARA can't help a small smile.

BARBARA: How gentlemanly of you.

HAROLD: I know. I even brought you a drink, but I see…

He gestures to the drink already in her hand.

I'm Harold.

BARBARA: Yes, I know. I've seen you around the library.

HAROLD: And you are…?

BARBARA: Barbara.

HAROLD: Beautiful name.

BARBARA: I've heard that one before, thanks.

HAROLD: I'm surprised to see you here. You don't strike me as the party type.

BARBARA: I'm not. Usually.

HAROLD: So why did you come?

BARBARA: I thought it would be fun, I suppose.

HAROLD: And is it?

BARBARA downs the rest of the drink she is holding, then swaps the empty glass for the drink HAROLD brought over for her.

A lady would say thank you.

BARBARA glares at him. He laughs.

You're funny, you know that?

BARBARA: *(Frustrated.)* Why do you do that?

HAROLD: Do what?

BARBARA: You laugh at everything. You don't take anything seriously.

HAROLD: I do.

BARBARA: Whenever I see you, you're just lording about, cracking jokes. And nicking all the best books.

HAROLD: What?

BARBARA: You know what I'm talking about. Basically everything having to do with Egyptian burial rituals. You took them all out over the summer before us new lot even got here. I asked the librarian. The only one that isn't checked out seems to have been marked as lost, and if you ask me, it seems downright fishy.

HAROLD: Egyptian burial rituals? Is that your sort of thing?

BARBARA: It's a fascinating subject.

HAROLD: I won't argue with you. I quite agree. How's this – I'll make you a deal.

BARBARA: What?

HAROLD: You can borrow whatever you want if you go out on a date with me.

BARBARA: No, thank you.

HAROLD: I'm not that bad looking.

BARBARA: That isn't the issue.

HAROLD: Well, that's a relief.

BARBARA: You want to know why I don't like you?

HAROLD: Tell me.

BARBARA: Because you don't know how to treat these things with proper respect.

HAROLD: They're just books.

BARBARA: And clearly you can't think of anything better to do with books than use them to pick up girls.

HAROLD: I beg your pardon?

BARBARA: You heard me.

HAROLD: I've spent a year and a half finding all my sources.

BARBARA: Well, you're willing to give them away awfully quickly.

HAROLD: You know what? Offer rescinded. You should just go ahead and recall all the books, and muck up my research. I'm sure that busy-body Librarian will be only too happy to help.

BARBARA: Well, maybe I will.

HAROLD: Good. I hope you enjoy them.

BARBARA: I will!

A small pause.

HAROLD: You know, I just came here tonight to have a good time.

BARBARA: So did I.

HAROLD: Well, you're really terrible at it.

BARBARA: Apparently, so are you. But I'm not here to go to parties, anyway. I'm not like some girls. I came to Uni to study.

HAROLD: So did I.

BARBARA: Oh please. Do you even give a toss about archaeology?

HAROLD: You couldn't begin to understand.

BARBARA: Go on. I'm curious.

HAROLD: Fine.

I study archaeology because it's like looking into the future. It reminds me every day how small we are. But we're part of a chain, connected to everything that came before, and we'll still be part of something even when we're gone. So if I laugh too much or smile too much, it's only because I think we ought to make the most of it while we're here. I apologise if my enjoyment of life offends you.

A small pause.

BARBARA: I was expecting one of the usual corny reasons about wanting to understand the history of man.

HAROLD: No. I have my own corny reasons.

BARBARA: I don't think they're corny.

I think they're true.

A quiet moment passes.

BARBARA: So now you don't like me, do you?

HAROLD: Well, I have to admit, you make it pretty damn difficult.

She smiles at him. He can't help but grin back at her.

BARBARA: Harold?

I might take you up on that offer about the books. If it's still valid.

HAROLD: Hmm. I'm afraid I'll have to get back to you about that.

BARBARA: Oh…

HAROLD: You see, you're not the only one interested in the offer.

BARBARA: Oh really?

HAROLD: You know Louis Fleming with the dripping nose? He's been after me for weeks. About the books, I mean. Lucky for you, he's not really my type.

BARBARA gives him a playful cuff on the arm. He catches her hand.

But you are. Exactly my type.

BARBARA: And what type is that?

HAROLD: The type who would fight me to the death over books about Egyptian burial rituals.

Come on. Let's dance.

I promise you, you won't regret it.

BARBARA: I know.

HAROLD and BARBARA begin to dance. The music rises to support them.

Members of the ensemble gradually join in – including the memory site team – until everyone is dancing.

Lights fade.

End.

OUR FATHER
by Deborah Bruce

All rights whatsoever in this play are strictly reserved and application for performance etc. should be made before rehearsal to United Agents, 12-26 Lexington Street, London, W1F 0LE. No performance may be given unless a licence has been obtained.

Characters

MARGARET
Not worked outside of the home since a secretarial job
and a little showroom modelling in her twenties. Brought
up her family, organised a family home, supported her
husband's public and high profile career and busy schedule.

JANE (Margaret's daughter)
Divorced. Fiercely strong work ethic. Runs her own
successful Interior Design company in Cape Town.
Mother, grandmother, efficient multitasker.
Organises people.

PENNY (Margaret's daughter)
Socialist. Labour MP for a West London borough for the
last twenty-nine years. Approaching retirement. At forefront
of feminist and environmental movements,
came up through CND in 1980s.
Never married, no children. Very private.
One hundred percent committed to the cause.

GEORGE II (Margaret's son)
Showed early promise as an actor appearing
in several films and a popular TV series but never
quite made it as his looks faded and his talent didn't quite
cut it. Has a natural charm and confidence
but an inner insecurity which holds him back.
Drinks too much. Rides on the coattails
of his father's celebrity.

SALLY (George II's wife)
Ex-model. Moderately successful in her time.
Sally and George II have three children; one married
and living and working abroad, one in and out of rehab, and
one killed in a motorcycle accident backpacking
round Thailand in his twenties.

CAROLYN DUKE
Family lawyer. Good at her job, a keeper of secrets.
Decent, strong instinct to do the right thing.

Scene Two
SUSAN
Worked in her local library all her life until library
services were cut and she was made redundant when the
library closed down two years ago.
She has battled hard to overcome difficulties with social
interaction, to hold down her job for so long.
Keeps herself to herself. A loner. Took over
parental role in the home after
the death of her mother.

ANNE
Cripplingly shy with strangers and hardly leaves
the house. A voracious reader. Collects autographs and
newspaper cuttings. Childlike enthusiasm
for popular culture and celebrity.

GEORGIE
Assistant technician in a chemistry lab at a London
University. Suspicious of public transport, he walks the
four miles to and from work every day.
Passionate ornithologist and
romantic dreamer.

JACKIE

Social worker. Worked with the family for years.
Moved departments, so no longer officially assigned
to them but feels attached.
Happily married to childhood sweetheart.

ROWENNA

A neighbour. She has known the family for thirty years.
Was a good friend to their mother and promised her
she'd keep an eye on them after she'd gone.
Never had children of her own but was a foster parent and
childminder. Her husband suffers from depression.

Scene Three

ELLEN

A very fabulous actress in the 60s and 70s.
A thrill seeker, a teenage spirit.
Twice divorced.

PAULA

Artist. Still exhibits and travels.
Her sons live close by and she is fully involved in
their lives with their wives and children.
Very easy-going, pilates, herbal teas, open to the world,
still curious and connected to new things.

MARTY

Costume designer for film and television.
Has enormous flair and bon viveur. Brilliant at luxury.
No responsibilities, no ties.
Battled a drink and drug problem in the 70s and 80s and
subsequently doesn't drink. He travels often,
still parties, has many friends of all ages.

JOY REYNOLDS
Freelance journalist
Longtime friend of Ellen's.

TIPPI (Ellen's daughter)
Head teacher of a primary school in a deprived
area of London. At the coalface of cuts to services
and the devastating effects they are having.
Married, one son, one daughter. About to
become a grandmother.

Our Father was first performed in the GBS Theatre at RADA on Saturday 12 December 2015.

DIRECTOR – Vivian Munn
DESIGNER – Miguel Guzman
MOVEMENT TUTOR – Angela Gasparetto
VOICE TUTOR – Caroline Kilpatrick
SUPPORT TUTOR – Ingrid Schiller

Cast
MARGARET – Sandie Barwick
JANE – Ruth Steele
PENNY – Jenni Wredden
GEORGE II – Richard Russell
SALLY – Himadri Babla-Jadhav
CAROLYN DUKE – Brigette Daniel
SUSAN – Ana Carrigan
ANNE – Vivienne Cove
GEORGIE – Donald Elliott
JACKIE – Judith Bevan
ROWENNA – Jeanie Deane
ELLEN – Yvonne Levy
PAULA – Marsha Myers
MARTY – James Banerjee
JOY REYNOLDS – Julie Davies
TIPPI – Diana Hudson
Due to the indisposition of Julie Davies special thanks goes to Anne Kavanagh

Production Team
STAGE MANAGER – Vari Gardner
DEPUTY STAGE MANAGER – Emily Melville-Brown
ASSISTANT STAGE MANAGER – Kelly Rosser
LIGHTING DESIGNER & OPERATOR – Daniel Smith
SOUND DESIGNER & OPERATOR – Nuno Rocha Santos

SCENE ONE

The large kitchen in MARGARET's house.

MARGARET's daughters PENNY and JANE are fussing around her with glasses of water and getting her to sit down. Her son GEORGE is hovering.

SALLY, GEORGE's wife, is sitting at the kitchen table looking through an old box of photographs.

PENNY: For goodness' sake, Mum.

JANE: Drink this, sit down.

MARGARET: I'm fine, stop it, I just stood up too fast.

PENNY: You're very pale. There's no need to keep standing up, we're all here, we can pass you things.

JANE: What have you eaten today?

PENNY: Yes, good question. She's not eating properly.

MARGARET: Yes I am, what are you talking about?

JANE: What did you have for lunch?

PENNY: When I rang the other night she hadn't even had supper. She said she'd had some Pringles and a yoghurt or something ridiculous.

MARGARET: That's because I'd had that big lunch with George and Sally, hadn't I?

GEORGE: At the Duke's Head? Yes, that was a lovely lunch.

PENNY moves away and starts to look through emails on her phone.

SALLY: *(Holding up a photograph.)* Where was this?

MARGARET: I had lunch, I finished the soup from yesterday.

JANE: Well what are you nearly fainting for? I think we should get you seen by a doctor, Mum.

PENNY: If you can ever get an appointment.

SALLY: Is this Cornwall?

MARGARET: I might have written it on the back, Sally, turn it over. Does it say?

SALLY: Yes – Cornwall 1976.

JANE: Why don't you go and have a lie down?

MARGARET: I can't have a lie down, Caroline Thing's coming isn't she.

PENNY: We can deal with that, we can tell you what she says afterwards, you could have a little sleep.

MARGARET: She said she wanted to speak to the whole family, I don't want a little sleep, there's far too much to do.

SALLY: *(Looking at a photograph.)* Oh no, somebody burn this, what on earth am I wearing!

JANE looks at the photo over her shoulder.

JANE: Dear god.

SALLY: I got that dress from a shoot, thanks everyone, for telling me I looked like a schoolgirl.

JANE: Let's not revisit that terrible day.

GEORGE: What is it?

JANE: My wedding.

MARGARET: Who to?

JANE: What do you mean, who to? Frank Palmer.

MARGARET: Well I can't see the picture.

JANE: I've only had one wedding, you don't need to see the picture.

PENNY: Is the wifi on?

SALLY: Everyone's name's on the back, that's a good idea.

We can't have been married then. Yes, my maiden name, look! Oh my.

JANE: And here you are, still here forty years on, for your sins.

GEORGE: *(Looking at the photo.)* Everyone's there except me. Where the hell am I?

SALLY: Flirting with the waitresses? Passed out under a table?

Awkward.

MARGARET: Maybe you were taking the photograph.

JANE: Of course he wasn't taking the photograph, we had a professional photographer, it was my wedding day.

Pause. JANE studies the picture.

JANE: Aaaw, look at Dad. So smart.

Look, Mum. Look at Dad.

The photograph is passed to MARGARET. She looks at it briefly.

MARGARET: Oh yes. He insisted on wearing that hat.

GEORGE: Always a hat!

Quiet. The photo is passed round.

PENNY: Dear old Dad.

JANE: Anyway. We're obviously not going to put a picture of my failed marriage on the order of service.

SALLY: Thank goodness for that!

JANE: Aren't there any of Mum and Dad when they were courting, or Dad in the Army? Before he was famous, that's what I was thinking. That's why I got the box down.

PENNY: Find one with all the family, Christmas day or something.

MARGARET: No moustache please.

PENNY: Not a public image, you know, just the family man. With a paper hat from a cracker or something.

GEORGE: He was a national treasure. We shared him with the nation.

PENNY: What a ridiculous thing to say. Of course we didn't. Not in any profound way. He was Dad. He was Mum's husband.

GEORGE: I'm going outside for a smoke.

He exits.

JANE: I don't know about anyone else but I might have to have a little snooze before supper, I can't shake this jet lag off.

MARGARET: What time is it for you then?

JANE: Only an hour ahead. I feel exhausted after the flight.

PENNY: Wouldn't really class it as jet lag then.

SALLY: I hope the solicitor lady comes soon, I've got a pedicure at four in West Hampstead.

Silence.

MARGARET: How about the picture of him and me outside his mother's garage when we got engaged and he was working at the BBC? Is that in the box?

SALLY: I'm getting wheezy from the dust on the lid. Can someone else take over?

GEORGE comes back in.

JANE: That was quick.

GEORGE: It's swarming with journalists outside.

MARGARET: You shouldn't be smoking out the front Georgie. They'll take a picture and put it in the paper and then Teddy will see it.

SALLY: Teddy's in rehab, they're not allowed papers there.

PENNY: Not allowed papers?

SALLY: Seeing a picture of his father having a cigarette is the least of his problems.

JANE: How's he doing?

SALLY: My poor Teddy, I can't talk about it.

JANE: Are they going to let him out to come to the funeral?

PENNY: Let him out? He's in the Priory, not Pentonville. Why aren't they allowed papers?

GEORGE and SALLY exchange a look.

GEORGE: We haven't actually told him, as such, about Dad.

JANE: Told him what, that he's died?

GEORGE: Not in so many words, no.

JANE: You haven't told him Dad's died?

GEORGE: He knows he's ill, of course. He knows he's probably *going* to die. At some point. We wanted to break it to him gently, he can't deal with big shocks.

SALLY: Teddy's in a dark place at the moment, Jane.

JANE: Mum? Did you know about this?

MARGARET: Well, if Georgie and Sally think it's for the best.

JANE: Aren't you worried he'll hear about it from someone else, what if one of the nurses mentions it, they will, surely.

SALLY: They don't call them nurses.

MARGARET: Someone should call Julian again, he needs to deal with the press. They shouldn't be outside the house today, they're supposed to be respecting our privacy.

JANE: What if they see his surname and offer their condolences?

SALLY: Georgie spoke to the support staff. They're under strict instructions.

PENNY: There's not much Julian can do, Mum. If they want to stand around outside, that's up to them, they're not on private property.

MARGARET: I don't want them here. They lean on the cars.

PENNY: Georgie.

GEORGE: What?

PENNY: Go and have a word with them.

GEORGE: And say what?

PENNY: Move them on. They're upsetting Mum.

MARGARET: They're supposed to be respecting my privacy.

GEORGE: You go, you're better at doing things like that. I'm too nice.

PENNY: You need to keep them sweet, you mean.

JANE: I'll go, I'm not too nice.

SALLY: Can't they stay, they're not doing any harm.

JANE: They're upsetting Mum.

GEORGE: What are you going to say?

JANE: That they're upsetting Mum so please can they piss off?

MARGARET: Don't say that Jane, they'll put it in the paper.

SALLY: Don't get on the wrong side of them, they'll write something unkind about Teddy.

PENNY: It's always been upside down, your relationship with the press, they know you need them, they've got you in the palm of their hand.

SALLY: I don't need them, what do you mean, need them?

PENNY: Every time you want a new kitchen, or a holiday, you sell them something. It makes you vulnerable.

SALLY: I don't tell them stories, they know things already.

PENNY: Come off it, how do they know? Who tells them then?

SALLY: *(Getting upset.)* I don't know who tells them, they just know. I can't help it if people are interested in my life. My looks thrust me into the limelight, this is the price I pay. Why's she picking on me? I don't invite it, do I Georgie?

GEORGE: I don't know, it all comes back to sex and money doesn't it.

JANE: What?

SALLY: What are you talking about?

MARGARET: If your father was here, he would see them off.

GEORGE: No he wouldn't! He'd throw his trilby on and get out there, big smiles, charm charm charm, who would like a drink? Taking them out on a tray. Peanuts in a little bowl. They loved him.

MARGARET: He'd see them off if I asked him to. He'd see them off now.

I can't believe he's gone. Suddenly that's it, a person's gone forever. It's so final.

JANE: I know.

PENNY: Oh Mum.

SALLY: I don't invite the attention. I'd love to be invisible like you.

JANE: I beg your pardon? I run my own company, I've got a twelve million pound annual turnover thank you very much. Penny's an OBE, we're hardly invisible.

SALLY: You're misunderstanding me. On purpose perhaps, it's OK, never mind.

Pause.

JANE: You OK Mum? Can I get you anything?

MARGARET: Pull the curtains in the front room, Jane, then at least they won't be able to see in.

PENNY: I'll do it.

MARGARET: And I can hear that wretched phone ringing in Dad's office, unplug it will you?

PENNY exits.

SALLY: Stifling in here. Is anyone else? I can't breathe.

JANE: Can I make you a little sandwich, Mum? Or a cheese biscuit?

SALLY: I could just about manage a drink but don't ask me to eat anything.

MARGARET: He said on television that time, do you remember? He was being interviewed by the Irish fellow and he said how he was a bad husband and a bad father because he was always working.

JANE: He wasn't though, was he, hey?

MARGARET: I was always in the shadows, but I was happy to be. I'm not a showy kind of person, he knew that.

JANE: He had enough showy at work, he'd come home to escape all that.

MARGARET: It's all downhill from now I suppose.

JANE: Don't say that, Mum.

MARGARET: All my friends say so. When your husband dies you're no one. You're not even a mother, just an obligation.

GEORGE and JANE exchange looks, roll their eyes.

The doorbell rings.

Who's this now?

JANE: It'll be Caroline Duke. Good.

GEORGE: What's she going to talk about, inheritance tax and death duties?

SALLY: *(Fans herself.)* As long as nothing is asked of me, I'll just sit here quietly and listen.

GEORGE: Couldn't she have done this over the phone, why do we all have to *be* here do you think?

JANE: Oh shut up Georgie, you were here anyway.

MARGARET: The whole family. She said she needed to speak to the whole family. Georgie, don't complain. I'm going to put the kettle on because she might want a cup of coffee.

JANE: Stay where you are.

MARGARET: Or tea, we've got some herbal tea because some people like that don't they.

Voices in the hall. PENNY comes in followed by CAROLINE DUKE. PENNY is carrying a large bouquet of flowers.

PENNY: Here we are.

CAROLINE: Hello Margaret.

CAROLINE greets MARGARET warmly and respectfully.

I'm so very sorry, you must be, well you must be in bits.

MARGARET: It's such a shock, even when you're expecting it, that's the thing.

CAROLINE: I can only imagine.

MARGARET: My son George is here.

GEORGE: Hello there.

CAROLINE: Oh hello, yes of course.

MARGARET: And my daughter's come over from South Africa.

CAROLINE: Hello.

JANE: Hello Caroline.

SALLY: Please don't be offended if I need to leave halfway through your little talk, I have an appointment.

JANE: Can I get you a coffee or a tea, Caroline?

CAROLINE: No, no. Please, I'm so sorry to intrude, I know what a difficult time this is, you must have lots to do, the preparations are all-consuming aren't they.

PENNY: There's lots of us, lots of delegating.

CAROLINE: And the press outside, that's not helpful, is it?

MARGARET: What beautiful flowers Caroline, there was no need.

CAROLINE: Oh no, they're nothing to do with me I'm afraid, they were being delivered as I arrived. I should have, I come empty-handed.

PENNY has opened a card that came with them.

PENNY: Aaah, sweet. Melvyn Bragg.

CAROLINE: Oh, but I have brought this though.

CAROLINE takes an award out of her bag.

George's Lifetime Achievement award from BAFTA, it's been in my office since February, I kept meaning to get it biked over.

MARGARET: It's a very ugly-looking thing, isn't it really, where can I put it where we can't see it.

JANE: Dad was always suspicious of these awards when other people got them, he said it's as if they're begging you to stop.

Laughter.

Like some terrible omen. Oh, yes it is ugly!

GEORGE: It's not that bad, I'll have it, I'll put it in my office.

PENNY: In your office! What do you do in there, read the paper?

MARGARET: Sit down, make yourself at home, have George's chair.

CAROLINE: *(Big breath.)* I'm going to stand if that's OK, Margaret. I feel more comfortable standing. If that's OK. I have to be honest with you, this is a slightly awkward – well, situation really.

MARGARET: Well, we're all here, like you said.

GEORGE: Is it OK if we sit down, or should we all stand?

CAROLINE: No, no, you do what you like. I'm just happier standing but please, you get comfortable.

JANE: Is it something bad?

GEORGE: Is it to do with death duties? Has it all disappeared in death duties? Because if my mother has to sell the house –

PENNY: Let's just listen.

CAROLINE: I have some information for you, that I need you all to hear. And I'm afraid that it might be confusing, and maybe a little unclear at this stage. I feel sorry, I regret, that this has to unfold in this way. I have to say, I have felt uncomfortable, I do hope you don't feel this is in any way disrespectful for me to say this Margaret, but I have been uncomfortable with this particular aspect of George's arrangements and, I feel a little compromised, as his solicitor. I did discuss this with him, on a couple of occasions, but he was resolute that this was how he wanted it. So, this is how it must be.

MARGARET: Yes, well. George was a very obstinate man.

Silence. Everyone waits.

CAROLINE: OK, so, I'm here to talk to you about George's will. Much of which I know you are familiar with, Margaret – in many ways it's as straightforward as you might expect. This house, the house in Spain, the house in Cornwall, all left to you, of course, Margaret, and to be divided equally, three ways, between your children, at the time of your death, it's all straightforward, all discussed and understood between you, I know that. The money too, I don't have the figures in front of me, but equal amounts for all four grandchildren, there are decisions to make, in due course, involving the sale of shares if you wanted to do that, of course that's entirely up to you, at a later date. All straightforward, as you would expect.

(Deep breath.) OK.

So now I need to talk to you all about a codicil George made, to his will, last year, soon after his diagnosis, and asked to be kept private until his death. And it falls to me, now, to impart some details of this, here, to you all, now.

JANE: Sounds ominous.

MARGARET: Would you like a herbal tea, Caroline? Did my daughter offer you a herbal tea? We have camomile, and peppermint. I think there's a red one too, cranberry is it Penny? Can you look? Or raspberry maybe?

CAROLINE: I'm fine, thank you Margaret.

PENNY: Mum, it's OK. We're all with you. We're all here.

SALLY: Georgie, open a window, it's so close.

GEORGE gets up, opens a window. Sits.

CAROLINE: So. This is in relation to a property George owned, another property, one that you may not be aware of. *(To MARGARET.)* A three-bedroom terraced house, in Shepherd's Bush, West London.

PENNY: Shepherd's Bush? That's in my area.

CAROLINE: Yes. George actually purchased this property for cash in 1954. And since then, there have been tenants living at the address. The alteration to the will stipulates that, in the event of his death, the tenants must be given three months' notice to vacate, the property sold, and the proceeds from the sale be kept separate from his other assets.

PENNY: Mum? Did you know about this?

CAROLINE: It's my understanding you weren't ever informed of the purchase of this property, Margaret, that's correct isn't it?

MARGARET: That's correct, yes.

GEORGIE whistles.

GEORGE: A three-bed in Shepherd's Bush, near the BBC is it? That's got to be worth a million? One and a half maybe.

CAROLINE: The property hasn't been valued yet. That will all go ahead in the next few weeks. Notice was served on the tenants today.

GEORGE: So the rent for this house? Was that being paid into Mum and Dad's account, or a separate account?

JANE: How did you not know about this Mum, I don't see how this can be.

MARGARET: We've never had a joint account, I just have my own account and Dad had his.

JANE: You don't have a joint account?

MARGARET: No.

CAROLINE: This is the thing, actually. There was no rent paid on the house.

JANE: No rent?

CAROLINE: No, that's the thing, no rent.

JANE: For sixty years, not ever?

GEORGE: How can they have got away without paying rent? This is ridiculous!

CAROLINE: Actually, there was no rent asked for on the property. The tenants were given the house rent-free.

SALLY: And you call yourself a lawyer! *(Laughing.)*

CAROLINE: Yes. It's an unusual situation really. It's – uncommon.

Pause.

PENNY: So, what was the situation? Was Dad giving this house as accommodation to people who couldn't afford a place to live? Did he set it up as a charitable organisation?

JANE: It sounds like a tax dodge.

PENNY: No, it sounds to me like a quiet act of philanthropy. Is that right?

CAROLINE: I don't think so exactly.

JANE: So it was a tax dodge.

CAROLINE: Not a tax issue, no.

PENNY: Right.

Pause.

Well in that case the obvious question we need to ask you now is – well! I feel afraid to ask it.

PENNY comes and stands behind MARGARET and puts her hands on her shoulders.

JANE: I'm not afraid to ask it. Who the hell lives in the house?

GEORGE: Quite.

JANE: Who the hell are they?

CAROLINE: OK, so the house was originally tenanted by a Mrs Baker, Sandra Baker, but she died in 2002 and since then her children, Susan, Anne, and George, have remained in the house. They remain in the house, and as I said, notice was served today.

PENNY: Do you know these people, Mum? I've never heard of any of them, have you?

MARGARET: No.

PENNY: Which street is this house on?

CAROLINE: Whitchurch Road.

PENNY: Yes, I know it.

(Beat.) Right. Sorry Caroline, this isn't making sense to us, so can you tell us the whole situation as you understand it, clearly, please. My mother's in a very vulnerable state, it's not fair to be oblique and make us read between the lines.

GEORGE: It seems very fishy to me, what was he playing at?

SALLY: Are they sex workers perhaps?

MARGARET: Sex workers?

JANE: Sally, thank you. Don't forget your appointment will you?

MARGARET: What's George got to do with a house of sex workers in Shepherd's Bush?

JANE: Nothing obviously, there will be a good reason for all this, we just don't know what it is yet. It's Dad! It's bound to be something sensible, something… nothing untoward, let Caroline explain it to us. We're not ourselves, Caroline, we're all over the place, we don't know anything about this house and our brains aren't fully functioning/ so if you'd just tell us the whole story.

PENNY: I'm going to take notes if that's OK, I've got my notebook, one minute.

PENNY finds her notebook in her bag and comes and sits down.

Right. Fire away.

Pause. As CAROLINE speaks, PENNY writes.

CAROLINE: Well. *(She is clearly very uncomfortable.)* Your father owned this house. These people live in it. Your father has altered his will to include the instruction that on the event of his death, this house is to be sold and the proceeds of the sale be kept separate and left to an anonymous recipient. This is all I can tell you. I'm sorry.

GEORGE: An anonymous recipient? Hang on.

CAROLINE: I don't know any more than that I'm afraid.

PENNY: *(Cold.)* You don't know, or you won't tell us? If you refuse to disclose anything that makes any sense, then why are you telling us any of it at all?

PENNY puts down her pen.

GEORGE: An anonymous recipient?

CAROLINE: Yes.

GEORGE: Is it one of us?

CAROLINE: It's not, no.

PENNY: A member of the extended family, is it?

SALLY: Is it Teddy?

JANE: Dad wouldn't leave a whole house to Teddy and nothing to Guy and Amanda.

95

GEORGE: Well, they're not here, are they? They didn't come and visit Dad like Teddy did.

PENNY: Dad wouldn't leave a house to Teddy, think about it.

CAROLINE: It's my understanding that the recipient is outside the family.

GEORGE: Outside the family? Who?

CAROLINE: I'm sorry, the information is very limited, but I did feel I wanted you to hear it from me. And now I must ask you to sign this letter stating that I have spoken to you about the change to the will – you don't all have to sign, just one of you, as a representative of the family – to say that I came here today and spoke to you all. I do apologise, I am very aware that this is not what you need right now. I feel uncomfortable.

PENNY: This doesn't make any sense. Does this make any sense to you, Mum?

MARGARET: Why do we have to sign a letter?

CAROLINE: It's a stipulation of the will. George asked that I informed you in person and I just need one of you to sign to say that I have.

Pause.

I am sorry, Margaret. I appreciate that this is hard.

MARGARET stands.

MARGARET: I want her out of my house.

CAROLINE: I understand.

PENNY: Mum, hold on.

MARGARET: I want her to leave.

GEORGE: She can't leave until she's explained who all these people are, the tenants and the anonymous recipient. How are these people connected to Dad?

SALLY: I've got a bad feeling about this whole thing.

CAROLINE: I will leave, of course. I understand. I just need one of you to sign this letter please.

MARGARET takes the letter and reads it.

Silence.

She signs it and hands it back to CAROLINE.

CAROLINE: Thank you.

CAROLINE gathers her stuff and, without making eye contact with anyone, she leaves.

No one speaks until the front door closes.

JANE: Well.

GEORGE: Mum. What does it mean?

JANE: I don't think you should have told her to go until she finished telling us all the details. That was quite rude.

MARGARET: What man makes his wife listen to his secrets and then sign a paper saying she's heard them, not three days after his last breath? What man does that?

Long silence.

JANE: There'll be a perfectly good explanation for all this. What Penny said about the charity work, that sounds the most likely.

SALLY: She said no.

JANE: Mum.

GEORGE: Who are these people? Why did Dad buy them a house?

JANE: Listen. Mum.

GEORGE: Why would he give a bunch of random strangers a house, he never bought us houses.

PENNY: He might as well have done, all the thousands he spent bailing you out over the years.

GEORGE: What's that supposed to mean?

PENNY: You've got a house haven't you, and how do you think you paid for it? You're hardly a workaholic.

GEORGE: I work!

PENNY: Doing what?

GEORGE: I'm writing my memoirs.

PENNY: God give me strength! You haven't worked since you were in your twenties and even then, I'm not sure I'd call hanging around on a film set in a wacky poncho work.

GEORGE: I still get royalties for that film, it's repeated all the time. I've never stopped working.

SALLY: I worked, thank you very much, *and* I brought up three children.

JANE: All the press outside, do you think they know something, do you think that's why they're sniffing around? Where the hell's Julian? Did he call you back, Mum? He's Dad's bloody manager for god's sake, why isn't he managing *this*?

GEORGE: People come up to me in the street all the time telling me how much they loved that film. All the time, strangers!

JANE: Those flowers, they arrived at exactly the same time as Caroline. Do you think they're bugged? Oh for God's sake, listen to me I'm cracking up.

SALLY: Not to mention I *lost* a child. Not that you would have *any* idea… The *strain* on a marriage. The horror.

Silence.

PENNY: OK well, I don't want to get into it all now.

PENNY moves into action, gathering her stuff, putting on her coat.

JANE: Where are you going?

PENNY: Into the office. I'm going to look these people up on the electoral role, I've been up and down Whitchurch Road hundreds of time, knocking on doors. Jane, can I leave you with the order of service, I said it would be with the printers by tomorrow morning. George, find a picture.

GEORGE: Don't tell me what to do, I'm not one of your constituents.

GEORGE pours himself a glass of wine.

SALLY pulls the box of photographs towards her and starts looking through it.

PENNY: Mum. What do you need? Are you going to be OK if I nip to the office for an hour?

MARGARET doesn't answer.

JANE: Of course she will.

PENNY: Mum? Don't worry, we'll sort this out. We'll get to the bottom of it. Oh dear, I wish Dad was here, so we could ask him. So much simpler!

JANE: I keep thinking he's going to just walk in through the door.

PENNY: And can you make Mum a sandwich or something?

JANE: The sound of his keys dropping into the silver dish, his briefcase down, hello darling! His smell, always a soft jumper. I wish he'd just walk in now, as if the last three days hadn't happened.

GEORGE: And I'd say, who the hell are these scroungers in this house in bloody Shepherd's Bush?

JANE: No Georgie, because that wouldn't have happened either. None of it. Just all back to normal.

GEORGE: Something's not right here. I'm not going to stand for this. That solicitor woman's making the whole thing up! No rent? The sale of the house going to an 'anonymous recipient'? She thinks we're a bunch of idiots, she's lining her own pockets, she's exploiting our grief, our vulnerability. What did the letter say, Mum, did you read it properly before you signed it?

The doorbell rings, followed by some gentle knocking.

PENNY: Now what.

GEORGE: You shouldn't have signed it.

JANE: Is it Julian?

PENNY leaves the room.

JANE: It might be Julian, he'll sort this out.

MARGARET moves the box of photographs towards herself and searches through it.

GEORGE: You should have your own solicitor, someone you can trust. I don't trust Caroline Duke, there's something duplicitous about her, the way she acts so gentle and sensitive, I mean, is she even a solicitor? She's like a pilates teacher, or someone who does face painting in a church hall, she's a charlatan.

GEORGE pours another glass of wine. The bottle is empty.

SALLY: What are you talking about? You string these crazy words together and say nothing.

PENNY re-enters.

PENNY: It's the pockmarked one from *The Sun*, I can see him through the glass.

JANE: Don't open the door.

PENNY: I didn't. It's obvious we're in here though, there's more of them arriving.

GEORGE: I'm going to Google that so-called solicitor and see what's what.

JANE: For God's sake, of course she's a solicitor! She deals with all of Dad's stuff, she's been a partner at Anderson and Scott for years, Georgie. If you want to do something useful, call Julian.

PENNY: I'm going to have to make a run for it, I'll have my car keys in my hand ready, head down, cold reptilian stare, I've been perfecting it over the years.

JANE checks her phone.

JANE: I don't know how you put up with it, all those awful men outside every day.

PENNY: Right, wish me luck. I'm going to the office. Mum, I'll be back in an hour or so. OK?

MARGARET holds a picture in her hand.

PENNY: OK Mum?

The doorbell rings.

Heaven's sake.

JANE: Don't be long, will you Pen?

MARGARET looks at the picture.

PENNY: Is that the picture you want on the order of service?

SALLY takes the picture out of MARGARET's hand.

SALLY: I don't think this is suitable really. *(To PENNY.)* It's just a load of people having dinner.

PENNY: Why don't you have a lie down for an hour, I can bring you a cup of tea when I get back?

MARGARET: That's her, on the left of him.

SALLY: Who?

SALLY looks at the picture.

MARGARET: I don't remember much about the evening, other than Jimmy Tarbuck was there. He was a lovely man, a gentleman. We were the only two ladies at dinner if I remember rightly. I can't recall speaking to her, or even noticing her. Just seeing her name, years later, written on the back of the picture there.

JANE takes the photograph from SALLY and looks at it. She passes it to PENNY who looks at it.

PENNY: It looks like a glamorous event, what was it, some awards thing?

PENNY turns the photograph over to look on the back.

She looks at the others.

She turns the photograph back over and stares at it.

GEORGE: What? What is it?

PENNY: It says Sandra Baker.

GEORGE: Let me see.

He takes the photograph and studies it.

SALLY looks too.

GEORGE: Why was she there? It's your writing, Mum.
You must know who she is.

MARGARET holds on to the back of a chair to steady herself.

MARGARET: Your father siphoned off the best of himself and
gave it to the world. He left us with the dregs.

PENNY: No Mum, don't say that.

MARGARET: The drinking. The depression. The spoilt child.

PENNY: No. That's not true. He went out into the world and
shared himself, yes, but he always came home to us.

JANE: Of course he did. He loved us.

MARGARET: Do you think so? Who knows?

JANE: I know.

Penny, you know too, don't you?

JANE takes the photograph.

PENNY: Yes of course. We all know. Don't we, Georgie?

Pause.

Georgie. He always came home to us, didn't he?

Silence.

MARGARET slowly, steadily walks out of the room.

Lights fade.

SCENE TWO

The late Sandra Baker's front room.

Her daughters, SUSAN and ANNE, are dressed very similarly to each other; her son, GEORGIE, wears a suit and bicycle clips. The three of them sit in a row like children summoned to be spoken to by a teacher. SUSAN has an open book on her lap. ROWENNA, their neighbour, stands by the door. JACKIE, a social worker, sits in an armchair reading a letter. A silence. Everyone is watching and waiting for her to finish.

JACKIE finishes reading the letter and looks at ROWENNA.

ROWENNA: Do you know what it means?

JACKIE: Well.

ROWENNA: I told you, didn't I? I said to my husband, I've never heard anything like it.

JACKIE: When did it arrive?

ROWENNA: Yesterday morning. That's right, isn't it Anne?

ANNE: Yes. It came through the letterbox.

ROWENNA: I didn't know who to call, I said to my husband, I should call someone but I don't know who.

JACKIE: Well I'm not strictly attached to the family anymore, you see. You know, since my hours were cut, I'm mostly in the office now, I'm only doing two half days you see. It's not strictly. My remit now.

ROWENNA: I see. Well I didn't know who else to call.

JACKIE: No that's fine. I'm happy to help out. I'll do my best.

Pause. JACKIE looks at the letter again.

GEORGIE: Chin up everyone!

ANNE: Be quiet Georgie. Jackie's reading our letter.

JACKIE: I'm a bit stumped, I must say.

ROWENNA: *(Nervous laugh.)* Join the club!

JACKIE: Out of the blue like this.

Pause.

GEORGIE: It's nothing we need to worry about, Rowenna, that's right isn't it?

ROWENNA and JACKIE exchange a glance.

ROWENNA: Oh no, nothing you need to worry about. Jackie and I are just trying to work it out, that's all.

GEORGIE: Because my programme's on at half past.

ANNE: Are you going to watch your programme, Georgie? While guests are here.

GEORGIE: Yes.

ANNE looks nervously at SUSAN.

ANNE: Oh, right-o.

Pause.

ANNE smiles at JACKIE.

ANNE: How long are you going to stay for Jackie?

JACKIE: Well, it's not a set time today because it's not strictly an appointment, so, I don't know exactly.

ANNE: Are you going to tell us about your cats?

JACKIE: I'm just having a look at your letter at the moment. But my cats are very well, thank you.

Pause.

Cagney had to go to the vet's last weekend because she got into a scrape with a neighbour's cat and ended up with a nasty tear on her ear so that was a bit of a drama.

ANNE: Is she better now?

JACKIE: She is yes.

ANNE: Good. We're going to get a cat one day. I've got nothing against dogs but I'd rather get a cat because I think cats are more independent. Well, it's been lovely chatting with you but I think I'll get on with my cutting and sticking now if that's OK with you Jackie.

JACKIE: Of course.

ROWENNA: I'd love a dog but my husband's allergic.

ANNE gets up and collects a scrapbook and some newspapers and scissors on a tray. She sits back down and gets to work.

SUSAN: So, basically, we shan't be leaving this house. Tell them that.

ROWENNA: Let's not jump the gun, Jackie's going to try and unmuddle it for us, aren't you?

SUSAN: Tell them we're too settled to move somewhere else. We've taken root here.

The doorbell rings.

ANNE: Ding dong Avon calling.

She laughs.

SUSAN gets up to answer the door.

ROWENNA: Where would they go? That's what I said to my husband. Where would they go? They've lived here longer than we have and we've been here since 1965.

ANNE: You're talking about us as if we're not here again Rowenna! *(Laughs.)*

ROWENNA: They can't just kick them out just like that. There's laws and all sorts.

JACKIE: A landlord is allowed to sell his property though, obviously.

ROWENNA: I've fostered over twenty children next door in that house! We'll all be here until we're carried out in our coffins, that's us!

ANNE: You have to have cardboard boxes now, not coffins, it's for the environment.

GEORGIE: Wicker baskets are OK too.

ANNE: Wicker baskets! *(Laughter.)*

GEORGIE: I saw it on TV-am.

ANNE: I'd be too nervous to get in!

GEORGIE: You wouldn't have any say in the matter would you, you'd be dead.

ANNE: Yes, well I suppose. *(Laughs.)* He's got a point there, hasn't he Rowenna.

ROWENNA: *(Laughs.)* Yes he has, can't argue with that can you?

SUSAN comes back in with a parcel.

GEORGIE: That for me?

SUSAN: Mr G. Baker.

GEORGIE: Let's have a look.

SUSAN gives him the parcel. GEORGIE looks at it very carefully.

ANNE: Tell them we can't move house because then how would they know where to bring Georgie's parcels.

GEORGIE: We'd change our address at the post office, there's a form you fill in. This looks like my *Birds of the Serengeti* with any luck.

GEORGIE struggles to open the parcel.

GEORGIE: I need to borrow your scissors Anne.

ANNE: I'm using them I'm afraid.

GEORGIE: Just for a moment.

ANNE: You'll have to be quick, I'm very busy.

ANNE reluctantly hands her scissors over. She holds them in the way you are taught to at school. She watches him use them, tutting a bit.

ANNE: OK, that's enough.

GEORGIE: I haven't finished.

ANNE: That's enough, you'll blunten them.

SUSAN: Who's the letter from? Is it legally binding? That's the question we have to ask ourselves. Would it hold up in a court of law?

JACKIE: It's from a solicitor. Representing the landlord.

ANNE snatches her scissors back.

JACKIE: Susan, do you have any paperwork relating to your tenancy or anything like that? Because I think that would be helpful.

ROWENNA: Well if they're anything like me, I can't find anything in my house. Would you even know where

to look, Susan? *(To JACKIE.)* Sandra wasn't the most
organised of people was she? I think that's fair to say.

ANNE: I think it's fair to say she was disorganised! *(Laughs.)*

GEORGIE: *Birds of the Serengeti*! Oh that's really super. Look at
that!

ANNE: Is it the book about birds of the Serengeti you ordered,
Georgie?

GEORGIE: Yes it most certainly is. Well, would you look at that!

GEORGIE reads the back of the book while the conversation continues.

'Located in northern Tanzania, / the Serengeti is one
of the world's most famous wildlife regions. *Birds of the
Serengeti* is a groundbreaking and essential photographic
guide, featuring more than two hundred and seventy bird
species most likely to be encountered in the Serengeti
National Park and Ngorongoro Conservation Area.
This easy-to-use guide includes four hundred and eighty
dazzling color photos, an attractive and handy layout, and
informative and accessible text that discusses interesting
behaviors and provides insights into species background.'
Well. What about that!

JACKIE: I'm sure there'll be a tenancy agreement somewhere
in this house, it's not the kind of thing you throw away.

SUSAN: It's the kind of thing I throw away.

JACKIE: Well, how do you pay your rent? Let's start there.

SUSAN: I don't think there's any need to get into all this.

JACKIE: Well housing's not my area of expertise but that's
where I'd start. If you can find your tenancy agreement, or
any documents relating to the rent and the conditions of
the rental, that's a starting point isn't it?

ROWENNA: Let's have a hunt around, shall we Susan? While Jackie's here to help you.

ANNE: Are you going to send an email about it, Jackie?

ROWENNA: Can you remember where you keep your bits and pieces about the house, Susan?

SUSAN: Let's think.

Pause.

ANNE: Are you thinking?

SUSAN: I'm trying to remember.

ANNE: Can you hear the cogs turning? *(Laughter.)*

Have you remembered yet?

SUSAN: I remember when our mother was alive, she used to open the curtains every morning and say, 'Good Morning World!'

ANNE: What did Lacey do when Cagney went to the vets, Jackie?

Pause.

JACKIE: Lacey died actually, Anne, sadly. Last November. Very peacefully. In her sleep.

ANNE: George Parish died, I'm cutting out all the obituaries, they're in all the papers.

JACKIE: Yes, isn't it sad, I read about that.

GEORGIE: And it was on the television.

ANNE: Oh yes, it's on the television at six o'clock and then at seven o'clock they say all the same things over again. They think people have very short memories, they must do.

JACKIE: Will you start a scrapbook on someone else do you think, now George Parish has passed away.

ANNE: I don't think so Jackie, it's a full-time job you see, and I'm not getting any younger.

ROWENNA: How many scrapbooks have you got on him Anne? You should see them!

ANNE: Thirty-four.

JACKIE: I have seen them, I remember from when I used to come on Tuesdays. It's quite a life's work.

SUSAN: There's an envelope in the filing cabinet upstairs in Georgie's bedroom with some paperwork in it.

JACKIE: That sounds like a good place to start.

ROWENNA: Shall I come and help you look?

SUSAN: I need to find the key first. Now. Where could that be?

GEORGIE: This really is a groundbreaking photographic guide!

ANNE: Is it really? Oh I am glad.

SUSAN: No. I can't think for the life of me where that key might be. I can picture it. Small and gold on a ring with an advert for Firestone tyres on it. My mind is falling away and the memories are all merging together! I try to think of the key and all I can think of is Mother opening the curtains!

JACKIE: I've got a pen and some paper in my bag, so what I'm going to do is start writing a list of the things that I think you need to gather together, so you can at least appeal against what it says in this letter.

ANNE: Was Cagney sad when Lacey died?

JACKIE: She was sad, yes. But Lacey had had a very happy life. So that was good.

ANNE: George Parish had a very happy life. And a long one. He had made over thirty programmes for the BBC and travelled all over Asia and Australia. He had a beer named after him in Sydney. He was a national treasure, that's what it says in all the papers. The nation held him close to its heart.

GEORGIE: Where are my binoculars?

SUSAN: Good Morning World!

Silence for a moment.

ROWENNA: Who'd like a cup of tea?

SUSAN, GEORGIE and ANNE all raise their hands.

ANNE: I'll have a T please Bob. *(Laughs.)*

JACKIE: Oh go on, I don't want to be the odd one out.

ROWENNA exits to the kitchen.

JACKIE finds a pen and paper in her bag and starts making a list.

ANNE cuts an article about George Parish out of the paper and sticks it in her scrapbook.

SUSAN moves closer to JACKIE.

SUSAN: *(In hushed tones.)* Please stop talking about the letter. It's upsetting Rowenna. She's worrying herself sick about this letter, we should never have shown it to her, it was a dreadful mistake.

JACKIE: I think Rowenna's just trying to help you.

ANNE: Her husband's a bully and a heavy drinker.

SUSAN: So you see this was all a big mistake.

ANNE: He's a depressive, he goes up to bed at ten to seven, it's not even dark. She's a slave to his moods.

GEORGIE: She does everything for him. He's the luckiest man in the world, but is he grateful?

ANNE/GEORGIE: No.

GEORGIE: What I'd do for a girl like Rowenna!

ANNE: You have to keep looking. *(Laughs.)*

GEORGIE: My heart! It's as heavy as a stone!

ANNE: Don't give up, she's out there somewhere!

JACKIE: I think Rowenna's worried for *you*.

SUSAN: We're as tough as old boots.

SUSAN takes the letter out of JACKIE's hands and rips it up.

ANNE: Hurray!

JACKIE: You need to take this letter seriously, Susan. You can't bury your head in the sand. I think we do need to find any paperwork you have, but even then, you know, your landlord does have the right to sell the house, if he wants to, as long as he gives reasonable notice.

SUSAN: No, it's all over now.

JACKIE: Not really, you have to face the facts.

SUSAN: I am very resilient. I have power and I have strength. When I lost my job in the library they put a letter in the envelope with my payslip. It said they were going to terminate my contract. I had worked for them for thirty-nine years and never been late once. They underestimated me. Our mother taught us to be invisible but she also taught us to be strong.

GEORGIE: I'm invisible at the lab, they say good morning and good night but no one speaks to me in between.

JACKIE: Are you busy at work at the moment?

GEORGIE: Oh yes, very busy.

JACKIE: Are you still walking to work every day?

GEORGIE: Oh yes, four miles there, four miles back.

JACKIE: I thought maybe you had got yourself a bike.

GEORGIE: No, still walking.

JACKIE looks at GEORGIE's bicycle clips, no explanation is forthcoming.

GEORGIE: I'm as fit as a fiddle, always have been and always will be.

ANNE: He'll make someone a good husband one day.

GEORGIE: Always courteous, polite, I try to put others before myself.

ANNE: *(Laughs.)* Well, he tries.

GEORGIE: I wash regularly, have many wide-reaching interests and hobbies. I can cook, I'm handy around the house. I nursed an injured bird back to health once, do you remember Anne?

ANNE: Yes.

GEORGIE: Do you remember Susan?

SUSAN: A little chaffinch.

GEORGIE: Mauled by a cat or a fox or something. I put it in a shoe box and fed it milk from a little pipette every three hours. We got on like a house on fire the two of us! Sorry to see him go when he eventually got strong enough to fly.

JACKIE: Sounds like you're a real-life James Herriot.

GEORGIE: So yes, you see. I'm all ready to find myself a nice wife and live happily ever after. Just waiting for the right lady to come along.

ROWENNA enters with teapot and cups on a tray.

ROWENNA: Tea time!

ANNE: It's all over now Rowenna, Susan has ripped up the letter, so everything's going to be alright.

ROWENNA: Oh I see.

ROWENNA pours the tea and everyone is quiet.

ANNE laughs nervously.

ANNE: All over now.

JACKIE smiles at her.

JACKIE: Have you managed to go out at all, Anne?

ANNE: No, I don't go out.

JACKIE: No.

GEORGIE: Anne doesn't like to go outside, do you Anne?

ANNE: No.

GEORGIE: She takes after our mother, our mother never went outside.

ROWENNA: Thirty-five years wasn't it, she never stepped foot outside the front door.

ROWENNA and JACKIE momentarily catch each other's eye. The ripped-up letter lies on the floor between them.

ROWENNA: Yes. And Anne's the spit of her mother too, aren't you Anne?

ANNE: Yes. We used to say, 'Spot the difference!'

Pause.

And Georgie's the spit of our father. Mother always used to say that, didn't she Georgie?

GEORGIE: She did, yes.

Everyone drinks their tea in silence.

JACKIE: When I was a girl, I moved house ten times between the ages of three and fourteen. My father was in the armed forces you see, he kept getting assigned to new postings and so my brother and I would have to uproot ourselves and change schools and make new friends. It wasn't easy. But even though each time I dreaded it, it was never as bad as I thought it was going to be.

No one says anything.

ROWENNA: Oh, how interesting.

Pause.

JACKIE: In fact. There's a few things that are really good about moving house.

Pause.

ANNE: Do you need someone to say, like what?

JACKIE: Yes, thank you! Well, like, making a new start and meeting new people is actually a really positive thing. And a change of scenery is a positive thing too.

ANNE: A change is as good as a rest.

JACKIE: Well, yes. That's it.

The doorbell rings.

ANNE: Ding dong Avon calling. *(Laughs.)*

SUSAN gets up to answer it.

ROWENNA: Well I've been here for all my married life.

JACKIE looks at her, a look that says, 'not helpful'.

But I've got nothing against moving. I'd like to live in Bristol. I went there once, it was lovely.

ANNE: No, we're happy here, thank you very much. Moving house is not for us.

SUSAN enters with a large tube.

GEORGIE: Is that for me?

SUSAN: Mr G. Baker.

GEORGIE: Look at the size of that, I say!

SUSAN hands it over.

GEORGIE investigates the package closely.

SUSAN: I'm going to plant a pyracanthus against that wall in the summer I think. Or a clematis.

GEORGIE: I tell you what, I think this may be the wildlife map I ordered from *The Telegraph.*

JACKIE: OK. *(To ROWENNA.)* I think what I'll do is go back into the office and have a chat with someone there about how to proceed with this.

ROWENNA: Well, I don't think they can expect them to move, not just like that, out of the blue. I don't think it's fair.

JACKIE: I'll see what I can sniff out as well, about this decision, where it comes from.

Pause.

You're ever so good to them Rowenna, they're lucky to have such a kind neighbour.

ROWENNA starts to cry.

ROWENNA: Oh dear I'm terrible when someone's nice to me, I'm not used to it you see, it knocks me off course.

ANNE: We made you a card last Easter didn't we, that said, 'Happy Easter to the World's best neighbour,' didn't it? And you cried then as well, didn't you?

ROWENNA: I can cry at anything. I cry at adverts. I cried at the one where the businessman throws his old mobile phone in the bin because he's getting a better one, and the poor old phone tries to scramble up out of the bin. Oh dear, it gets me every time. I can feel myself going now.

ROWENNA composes herself.

I think such a lot of them, you see. Nevermind me being the world's best neighbour, there's nothing these people wouldn't do for anyone. Anne can't go out, fair enough, but she'll put the kettle on and make me a hot drink as soon as look at me. Susan's set in her ways, but she's kindness itself. And Georgie, well, what a lovely lad. Always has been. No side to him, just decency through and through.

GEORGIE blows her a kiss.

And I promised Sandra, you see. 'Sandra,' I said, 'I'll keep them right. Have no worries on that front.' I take bits of washing through on a Wednesday, bring them their tea on a Friday sometimes, after I've done the big shop. We joke about it. We say, hark at us, we're like that television programme about the neighbours in Australia, what's it called?

JACKIE: *Neighbours*, do you mean?

ROWENNA: That's the one. It's like *Neighbours*, we say, but without the good weather! *(She laughs.)*

That bastard. Selling the house. What a thing to do.

Pause.

JACKIE: Who?

ROWENNA: Oh ignore me, I'm just. Ignore me.

Pause.

SUSAN stands as if struck by a thought. She leaves the room.

JACKIE: Why did their mother stop going out of the house do you think? Was she a very nervous woman?

ANNE: You're talking about us as if we weren't here again.

JACKIE smiles.

ANNE: It's OK. I'm busy with my scrapbook anyway.

ROWENNA: She got stuck in her ways. Time passes and things harden around us like cement, don't they. Before you know it, you're a person who never goes out.

GEORGIE: She went out to go to her funeral didn't she. There was no getting round that.

ANNE: I didn't go.

GEORGIE: You came later.

ANNE: I didn't think I'd be able to go but then when everyone had gone, I felt so small in the house all by myself. I was scared I was going to disappear altogether. So I put on my mother's coat and ran all the way to the church. And the service had already started and I was afraid to make a scene so I thought I'd go and sit on a bench in the porch. And as I sat there, a car pulled up and stopped outside the gate, and in the back seat, I saw George Parish. He got out and stood at the gate, staring, his hand on the collar of his coat. He had a signet ring on his little finger. I recognised it from *George Parish Looks Back at The Week.* He lifted his hat off his head and just stood there looking right at me. And I remember thinking, am I really here, did I really run all the way to the church in my mother's coat or am I actually still at home feeling small?

Silence.

ROWENNA: Fancy that. Seeing George Parish like that. Well I never.

JACKIE: Was it after that you started doing your scrapbook?

ANNE: Georgie! You're missing your programme!

GEORGIE: Oh my goodness, I've been so wrapped up in my parcels I've lost track of the time!

ANNE: He's lost track of the time!

ROWENNA: I lost track of the time years ago.

GEORGIE puts his parcels away and locates the remote control.

SUSAN returns with a large envelope in her hand.

JACKIE: Oh well done you, have you found your tenancy agreement?

ROWENNA: Did you find it Susan?

SUSAN: There's no tenancy agreement. Nothing written down. Remaining invisible was our mother's sole occupation, it was her area of expertise. You won't find any evidence in this house of my mother's existence other than our memories of her.

SUSAN holds the envelope out to JACKIE.

SUSAN is shaking.

So here, our birth certificates. Evidence of *our* existence. We exist. No one can deny that, it's written here in ink.

JACKIE doesn't take the envelope.

JACKIE: Well, thank you Susan, but I don't think your existence is in dispute here. This isn't about your existence, really.

SUSAN: *(Intense.)* We have a right to be here.

JACKIE: Yes, but the landlord also has a right to sell his house you see.

ANNE and GEORGIE are very still and shocked by SUSAN.

It would help if we knew who the landlord was. Do you know his name?

Everyone looks away.

Silence.

The doorbell rings.

ANNE: *(Quietly.)* Ding dong Avon calling.

SUSAN leaves the room.

Pause.

ROWENNA: Georgie Baker! You and your parcels!

Pause.

JACKIE: Listen. Don't worry. We'll sort this out and whatever happens, it's going to be alright. OK?

SUSAN returns, followed by PENNY PARISH.

ANNE, in the company of a stranger, physically shrinks.

PENNY is nervous but putting on a face.

PENNY: Hello. Hello.

ROWENNA/JACKIE: Hello.

PENNY: Hello. I'm so sorry to bother you. I'm. I'm
Penny Parish, you might know me. I'm the MP for
Hammersmith. I don't know if you – I'm your local
MP – I –

*PENNY looks at GEORGIE. She stops speaking and stares. She feels
faint, she tries to start speaking again but can't. PENNY is staring
at GEORGIE. Everyone is staring at PENNY.*

After a moment, GEORGIE jumps up and offers her his seat.

GEORGIE: Here, sit down.

PENNY sits. She looks intently at GEORGIE, her mouth dry.

PENNY: Thank you, I'm sorry. I feel a little strange, it's the
heat I think, I've been knocking on doors. I –

I.

I've been knocking on doors. Speaking to people.

I.

Everyone is staring at PENNY.

She tries to compose herself.

She has no voice.

SUSAN stands tall with the birth certificates in an envelope in her hand.

Slow, slow fade to black.

SCENE THREE

ELLEN's bedroom in a penthouse flat in Knightsbridge, where she lives with her friends, PAULA and MARTY.

ELLEN is in bed. She is wearing a black nightdress and a black scarf around her head. PAULA sits on the edge of the bed holding her hand. MARTY stands in the doorway of the room.

PAULA: We went on your walk. We missed you! It was no fun without you. Was it Marty?

MARTY: No fun at all. No bitching. No swearing.

PAULA: No hip flask of gin.

MARTY: God it was dull!

ELLEN smiles weakly.

PAULA: I wish you would talk to us darling, it's awful seeing you like this.

ELLEN: I don't have words Paula.

PAULA: I know.

ELLEN: Be patient with me, I need to process it myself.

PAULA: Of course. It's OK. Take your time.

We're here for you, you know that, as soon as you need to talk.

MARTY: Did she say no to tea?

PAULA: Did you want tea, darling? Marty's making a pot of lovely tea.

ELLEN: Maybe later.

MARTY exits.

PAULA: What time's Tippi coming?

ELLEN: She'll be so angry with me.

PAULA: No. What for?

ELLEN: Making a fuss. She's got an Ofsted coming up.

PAULA: She won't be angry with you. You're grieving, you're in shock.

ELLEN: It's just so painful, Paula. Loving someone, being loved back, and then losing them.

PAULA: I know.

MARTY comes into the doorway with a cup of tea.

ELLEN: And not being allowed to grieve. Not having any right to mourn for them.

MARTY: That's a mistress's lot I'm afraid.

PAULA: Marty.

MARTY: It's true. A mistress isn't welcome at a family man's funeral is she, nobody wants that.

ELLEN: He's everywhere. Pictures of him in the paper and footage of him on the news. It makes it so much harder that I can't speak of our love.

MARTY: Everyone loved George Parish.

ELLEN: Twenty years, my secret happiness.

MARTY: George Parish belonged to them all.

ELLEN: He was my heart.

MARTY: He was everyone's heart.

ELLEN starts to cry.

PAULA: I'm not convinced you're making this better, Marty.

MARTY: I'm just speaking the truth. I'm a plain speaker, Ellen knows I love her, don't you darling?

ELLEN: Yes.

PAULA: Perhaps you could love her without making her cry.

MARTY: She's got enough yes-men around her, the silly old cow. What did they call you in *Hello*?

ELLEN: Vintage.

MARTY: *(Laughs.)* That's right, Vintage Beauty Ellen Cosgrove. You get enough of that nonsense, you don't need us buttering you up at home.

So yes. You had your fun, you got away with it. Now it's time for the shitty end of the stick, you don't get to share your pain. You have to stand in the wings and watch. You do your grieving in secret. This is the price.

The buzzer goes.

MARTY: And here's your daughter come to terrorise us all. Happy days.

He goes to answer the intercom.

MARTY: *(On intercom.)* Thank you Marek, send her up.

Right. Hard hats on. The wrecking ball's here.

MARTY exits.

ELLEN: Don't leave me on my own with her, she'll shout at me.

PAULA leaves the room.

Where are you going?

PAULA: *(Calling from off.)* I've just remembered my hairdresser had a smoke on the balcony, I'm just going to make sure

125

he didn't leave a cigarette butt anywhere, in case Tippi finds it.

ELLEN is by herself.

She quickly sits up and takes a letter from her bedside table and hides it under her pillow. She lies back down again.

After a moment we hear TIPPI in the hall coming into the flat, calling 'Hello'.

She is greeted by MARTY and PAULA calling 'Hello' back. There is another voice too: JOY, a friend of ELLEN's.

TIPPI comes into the bedroom.

ELLEN: *(Weakly.)* Hello darling.

TIPPI: What are you in bed for?

ELLEN: I can't face getting up.

TIPPI: Don't be silly, you can't stay in bed all day, you'll get bed sores. Joy's here. I met her at the lift.

ELLEN: Is she? What a surprise.

TIPPI: She said you told her to come. What are you up to?

ELLEN: Nothing! What do you mean? Why can't my friend come and visit me without me being up to something?

TIPPI: She's not your friend, she's a journalist. What are you up to? I know you inside out, you can't manipulate me like you can everyone else.

ELLEN: Don't be nasty to me darling, I have a physical pain in my heart, I feel as if it could crack open any minute.

TIPPI: Why are the curtains closed? It's the middle of the day.

ELLEN: *(Calls.)* Paula!

126

TIPPI: What's that terrible smell?

PAULA enters.

TIPPI blows out a scented candle on the bedside table.

ELLEN: Come and sit in here, Tippi's bullying me.

PAULA: *(Smiling.)* Oh Tippi, how could you, your poor old Mum.

TIPPI and PAULA kiss hello.

TIPPI: Has she got you and Marty running rings around her?

PAULA: The poor love, it's hit her hard.

TIPPI: Don't be fooled.

ELLEN: You behave as if I'm some hard-hearted witch.

TIPPI: No comment.

MARTY appears in the doorway.

MARTY: Can I get anybody anything?

ELLEN: Where's Joy?

MARTY: In the bathroom.

Tippi, anything for you? Tea, coffee? The fresh blood of a virgin?

TIPPI: Just a glass of water please Marty.

MARTY: Yes, Ma'am.

MARTY bows and exits.

TIPPI: *(To ELLEN.)* Where did you get this ridiculous nightie from?

ELLEN: It's my nightie.

TIPPI: No, you've bought it specially haven't you? Is Joy doing an interview? You haven't got a photographer coming have you?

ELLEN: Of course not! It's just an old nightie.

TIPPI: It's still got the labels on. You are definitely up to something. I'm too busy for any nonsense today, Mum. I've got an Ofsted starting tomorrow, I've got no time for silly games. I shouldn't even be here.

ELLEN and PAULA exchange a look.

PAULA: Oh Tippi, you are being a bit hard on her.

ELLEN: George has died, darling. I'm in shock.

TIPPI: I know Mum, and that's sad. But I can't help thinking it's even sadder for his wife and their children. Right. Get up.

JOY enters, followed by MARTY with some red roses in a vase.

JOY: Ellen. I brought you these. Marty's arranged them in a pretty vase. Look. I thought of you as soon as the news came into the office, I thought oh, poor poor Ellen, she'll be feeling wretched. And so alone.

JOY takes in the room full of people.

How lovely everyone's here. But you can feel you're most alone surrounded by people can't you? I was so glad when I got your text. I was supposed to be doing an interview with Ulrika Johnson, she's having an ugly dispute with a neighbour over a parking space, but I dropped everything and jumped in a cab.

TIPPI: My mother cannot be a story, Joy.

JOY: Of course not, I'm here as a friend.

TIPPI: I have an Ofsted, I need one hundred percent focus
from my staff and parents, I can't be dragged into a
grubby association/

JOY: Please.

TIPPI: You cannot write a single word about my mother's
relationship with George Parish. He's dead. It's over.

JOY: I'm sorry Tippi, I don't want to fall out with you of all
people, but/

TIPPI: There is absolutely nothing to be gained from digging
it all up and raking over it now.

ELLEN: Joy's been my friend for nearly twenty years, Tippi,
do try not to insult her.

JOY: I've never breathed a word to a single soul about
Ellen and George Parish. I'm very clear about keeping
friendship separate from work.

TIPPI: Mum. What's going on?

JOY: Look, I brought flowers.

TIPPI: I know my mother inside out, she's up to something.
What did you text Joy for?

ELLEN: Oh my heart, the pain's running all the way down my
right arm now.

TIPPI: No it's not. Sit up.

PAULA: Shall I call the doctor, Ellen?

TIPPI: Don't be ridiculous, I've got a Rennie in my bag, she
can have that, she's fine.

ELLEN: I can't get my breath, I feel lightheaded.

TIPPI: Stop it.

DEBORAH BRUCE

PAULA: She does look terribly pale Tippi, are you sure
    I shouldn't call someone?

TIPPI: She's fine, she's just reeling off a list of heart attack
    symptoms, she'll have seen them on Facebook or
    somewhere. Mum, sit up, come on.

TIPPI pulls ELLEN up and plumps up her pillows. She finds the letter.

She holds it up and looks at ELLEN.

ELLEN and JOY look guiltily at each other, then sheepish.

TIPPI: I knew it.

    What's this?

Pause.

ELLEN: *(Very quietly.)* George has left me his house.

TIPPI: What? Speak up, I can't hear you.

ELLEN: George has left me his house.

TIPPI: He's left you his house? His family's house?

ELLEN: Not his family's house, no, another house. A spare one.

TIPPI: A spare house?

ELLEN: Yes.

TIPPI: What for? You don't need a house.

TIPPI opens the letter and starts reading it.

PAULA: You're not going to leave us and live in it are you?

ELLEN: He's selling it, he's giving me the money. I got
    the letter this morning from his solicitor, I rang her
    straight away.

TIPPI: Rang Joy straight away more like. I *knew* you were up to something.

ELLEN: She's coming to see me. George left a special, secret will. He never even mentioned it. It's the kindest, most romantic thing anyone's ever done for me.

Pause.

I was going to tell you.

PAULA: When did you get the letter, Ellen?

ELLEN: This morning, when you and Marty went for your walk.

PAULA: But the post arrived before we went for the walk, you must have got the letter before we left, you said you didn't want to come, that you were going to try and sleep. Why didn't you tell us about it? We tell each other everything don't we, no secrets. It's in our contract, remember.

ELLEN: I was going to tell you.

PAULA: I see.

ELLEN: When you got back.

PAULA: So you texted Joy while me and Marty were out for the walk, did you?

ELLEN: Maybe, I'm not sure exactly.

PAULA: Telling her about the letter and the secret will, and asking her to come round.

ELLEN: Well yes, I think I must have done.

PAULA: Right. I see.

Pause.

JOY: Come on Paula. Let's be grown up about this. It's a no-brainer. The press are sniffing around this already. Ellen's

131

got no choice, she has to put her side of the story out there or someone else will just make it up.

MARTY: You're going to talk publically about your relationship with George Parish? In the *Mail*?

JOY: The press have held the story for years, they knew exactly what was going on. If she doesn't talk about it, they'll go with it anyway. Parish struck a deal with them, didn't he. Come on, don't be naïve, this is how it works.

He threw them little scraps along the way, his son's affair with his personal trainer, his grandson's spells in rehab, his daughter's failed marriage, all sorts of stories to keep them off his back, feeding them just enough to stop them from starving, keeping them in his pocket so they didn't blab about Ellen.

The picture library's full of images of George and Ellen arriving at hotels in taxis and leaving restaurants through the kitchen.

He's dead, Ellen's vulnerable. They've got all the content, it's ready to go.

She has to take control.

Pause.

MARTY: But everybody loves George Parish.

JOY: I know. He's going to get a bit knocked off his pedestal, it's par for the course.

PAULA: And what about his family?

JOY: An inevitable fallout. C'est la vie.

Pause.

MARTY: I'm not going to lie to you, Ellen, I'm shocked you're going to go public with this.

ELLEN: Why? I want the world to know he loved me.

MARTY: Why do you need the world to know that?

ELLEN: Because he was mine. And I loved him.

MARTY: He wasn't yours, isn't that the point? And love is private, surely. It's not very classy, is it?

ELLEN: I'm not strong like you, I can't do it. The pain of losing him is too hard to bear by myself.

MARTY: You're not by yourself, though, are you?

ELLEN: 'Even in a crowd, you are alone inside your own head.'

TIPPI finishes reading the letter, folds it and puts it back in the envelope.

TIPPI: Right.

When you've finished coming up with a new range of slogans for Clintons cards. Listen carefully.

We're going to do a new thing. It's called putting the needs of others before our own. I understand this is an entirely novel concept for you, I don't expect you to grasp it straight away. I'll take you through it slowly.

You are not accepting a single penny from the sale of this house. This house is not yours.

As alien a thought as this might be, this is not all about you.

George Parish had a wife. He had children. He had grandchildren. He has an obligation to them, not to you.

George Parish may have felt like your special person, and I do appreciate that having a special person is a wonderful and precious thing, but he was not yours.

How would I have felt, when Dad died, if some woman popped up and started laying claim? Devastated.

Not to mention, George Parish chose a career path that comes with certain responsibilities. He represented something. He represented integrity. He represented good old-fashioned family values, salt of the earth, decency and truth. And as ironic and ludicrous as that may be, that's precious; and I don't want you and Joy smashing it into tiny pieces and ruining it for everyone.

MARTY: *(Gives short round of applause.)* Well said.

JOY: Marty! You of all people. I thought you were all for calling a spade a spade.

MARTY: I am.

But I've loved, and I've lost. And I know none of us have much, really, to hold on to. Some things feel sacred. We have to protect them.

JOY: So naïve! It's a sham. Why protect a falsehood?

PAULA: I know what you're talking about, Tippi. It's the desperate, crashing disappointment of it all that erodes us away. I don't know if we can bear any more of it, can we?

The buzzer goes.

ELLEN: Oh no, that'll be her! The solicitor! Send her away Paula, I can't see her yet, I'm all confused now, I don't know what to say.

TIPPI walks into the hall, she can be heard on the intercom.

TIPPI: *(Off.)* Thank you Marek, send her up.

ELLEN: Paula, please, say I'm too weak to see anyone, say something to make her go away.

PAULA: I can't, Ellen. Tippi won't let me.

The four of them sit in silence.

After a moment.

JOY: I saw your exhibition, Paula, I went with my daughter, it was beautiful.

PAULA: Oh! Thank you.

MARTY: You're quite the culture vulture aren't you?

JOY: I studied Fine Art at St Martin's actually. Back in the day.

MARTY: My! And now you write for the *Mail.* What a diverse contribution you've made to the world.

JOY: You're a terrible snob Marty.

TIPPI can be heard in the hall greeting CAROLINE DUKE.

TIPPI enters followed by CAROLINE.

TIPPI: Please forgive my mother, she's trying on a new role for size. It involves her being in bed. I do hope you can see past this rejection of social norms.

CAROLINE: That's no problem at all, I completely understand.

Hello Miss Cosgrove, it's a great pleasure for me to meet you. I'm a big fan of your work. I went to see *The Chance* about six times when I was a student at Warwick.

ELLEN: So pleased.

TIPPI: My mother is unable to accept Mr Parish's offer.

CAROLINE: I beg your pardon?

TIPPI: She doesn't want the house, thank you so much.

135

CAROLINE: Mr Parish stipulates in his will that the house must be sold, so it's the proceeds from the sale that are left to your mother in his will.

TIPPI: Yes we understand, she doesn't want them.

ELLEN: Please Tippi, can I keep it? I could donate some of it to charity, I could put a tiny bit of it towards a roof terrace, you know how much I'd like one. George wanted me to have one.

TIPPI: You've got plenty of money, you can build a roof terrace if you want one.

ELLEN: But it would be such a lovely symbol of our love if George bought it for me, a secret garden looking down over the city, no one knowing I was there.

TIPPI: *(Ignoring ELLEN. Speaking to CAROLINE.)* It invites too much attention, it comes with too high a price, she can't accept it. We'd like to pass the money straight back to his family where it belongs.

CAROLINE: OK, well. I'll need instruction from Miss Cosgrove if I'm to take this further. Mr Parish states very clearly that the money is to go to her.

TIPPI: Mum, can you instruct. Thank you.

I'll put it in writing for you.

TIPPI starts to type into her iPad.

ELLEN: What do you think, Paula? You'd like George to buy me a roof terrace, wouldn't you? Marty? We could sit out there in the evening and watch the sun go down. A nice G and T. We could talk about the good old days. I could remember George.

MARTY: I've said what I feel darling, you're an intelligent woman, you know what to do.

PAULA: I think you need to do the right thing.

ELLEN: Eurgh, the right thing's so *dull*.

PAULA: See it as protecting George from himself. It can't all blow up, can it Joy, if she's not left the money?

JOY: It won't make a huge difference, the affair story's still live.

PAULA: But if the money goes straight to the family, that's not a story is it?

MARTY: 'Proceeds from sale of house go to immediate family,' not a headline, surely.

JOY: I suppose.

PAULA: And some old pictures of people getting out of a car isn't a story.

JOY: Pictures of George Parish and Ellen Cosgrove getting out of a car and into The Hilton is a story.

MARTY: But it's a non-story. They were having a meeting, Ellen was considering appearing on George's show. They left out the back to avoid exactly this kind of childish, tabloid speculation. He's happily married for God's sake.

ELLEN: Maybe I could have a bit of the money, but not sell the story. Joy? Can you keep it quiet for me?

JOY: A will's a public document. It'll pique interest, you can only control so much.

MARTY: Your conscience is in your power to control.

TIPPI: *(Holds up her iPad.)* Where's your printer on this list?

ELLEN: I don't have my glasses, I think it's a Breville.

PAULA: That's the juicer. It's the Epson.

TIPPI: Right. Print.

DEBORAH BRUCE

CAROLINE: Obviously I'd need to work this document up and send it to your mother.

TIPPI: Of course, I just want to get something signed now so no one can change their mind.

CAROLINE: May I?

TIPPI gives her the iPad.

CAROLINE reads from TIPPI's screen.

'The children of George Parish,' that's fine.

TIPPI: I don't know who they are. Except that awful MP.

JOY: Penny Parish. Piranha Parish they call her at the paper.

MARTY: And the alcoholic actor son from those inane films.

JOY: George Junior. Poncho Parish.

CAROLINE: Yes, no need to write in names. I'll sort that out.

MARTY: There's three of them aren't there?

JOY: Yes. There's one in South Africa.

CAROLINE: Leave it with me.

JOY: None of them short of a few quid I should think. He must have left them their share.

TIPPI: Not our business.

CAROLINE: There's six of them actually. Mr Parish had six children.

JOY: Really? Are you sure? I didn't know that.

CAROLINE: Not many people do, but yes. George Parish had six children.

Beat.

So. You can leave the details to me. I'll do the right thing.

Pause. JOY makes a note.

TIPPI: Jolly good. Now if everyone wouldn't mind giving my mother a bit of privacy, she's going to get up and dressed now.

CAROLINE: Yes, of course.

CAROLINE gathers her stuff and prepares to leave.

TIPPI: Where's the printer? Is it in your studio, Marty?

MARTY: It is, darling, yes.

TIPPI marches out with her iPad. CAROLINE follows her.

MARTY: Will I get a detention if it's in a mess?

MARTY exits after her.

Silence.

PAULA smoothes the bedspread.

JOY checks her phone.

JOY: Ooh, I just need to cancel the photographer.

JOY makes a call.

PAULA clears a few cups and papers and exits.

JOY: *(On phone.)* Sorry, Denis? Joy.

JOY exits blowing kisses and waving.

Alone, ELLEN gets up and sits on the edge of her bed.

After a moment TIPPI comes back in, officiously holding paperwork and a pen.

TIPPI gives ELLEN the pen and holds the papers out for her to sign.

ELLEN: Can I sleep on it Tippi? Think about it a bit.

TIPPI: Sign.

ELLEN reads and reluctantly signs. And another.

Sign.

ELLEN signs. And another.

Sign.

ELLEN: Hang on, it's too fast, I'm not even getting a chance to read these.

TIPPI: It's all the same thing. Three copies of the same letter. Sign.

ELLEN signs.

ELLEN: I could be signing anything here. The deeds for my own execution.

TIPPI: You are ridiculous, Mother. You've always suffered from acute self-importance.

TIPPI puts the papers in a plastic envelope.

I don't think you've ever really grasped the concept of your own insignificance, have you?

ELLEN: Who wants to grasp that? Being significant is all I've ever strived for. It's all everyone strives for, isn't it? For God's sake darling, don't deprive us of that.

Pause.

TIPPI: Right, I'm off.

ELLEN: Oh, you're going, thank God.

TIPPI kisses ELLEN on the forehead.

TIPPI: Aren't you going to say good luck?

ELLEN: What for?

TIPPI: The Ofsted. It's a big deal.

ELLEN: Oh yes, of course darling, good luck, I hope you win.

TIPPI rolls her eyes.

Get Paula to come and sit with me will you, I don't want to be on my own.

TIPPI exits.

ELLEN sits. She takes a necklace from her bedside table and puts it round her neck.

After a moment PAULA enters.

Fasten this catch for me will you, I can't do it.

PAULA: Of course.

PAULA comes behind ELLEN and fastens her necklace.

Did George give you this?

ELLEN: Yes.

PAULA: Isn't it beautiful. Very you.

It's fastened.

There.

PAULA sits on the bed.

ELLEN: I don't even know when the funeral is. I'll call Julian, he'll tell me. Not that I'll be able to go. You'll stay with me won't you.

PAULA: Of course.

ELLEN puts her hand on the necklace.

ELLEN: He chose this for me all by himself, I didn't point him in the right direction even. That's the sort of man he was, you see. Attention to every detail, noticing everything about people. No one knew him like I did. Such a good, kind man. So thoughtful. And selfless. Always knew what to do, he took control, he shielded me from everything.

I'm frightened, Paula.

PAULA: Don't be frightened. What are you frightened of?

ELLEN: Drowning.

PAULA: No!

ELLEN: Pass me his picture.

PAULA passes her a picture in a frame from her dressing table.

ELLEN looks at it.

My George. Protecting me.

Now he's gone. The floods will come.

Slow fade to black.

End.

THE WORD
by Nell Leyshon

All rights whatsoever in this play are strictly reserved and application for performance etc. should be made before rehearsal to United Agents, 12-26 Lexington Street, London, W1F 0LE. No performance may be given unless a licence has been obtained.

Characters

(all remain on stage for the whole show)

EVA

PETER

(Eva and Peter are a couple. They met when they
were twenty, have been together ever since.
They have three children.)

JUNE

ROBIN

(June and Robin are a couple. They met two years ago,
both were divorced. Both have children
and grandchildren.)

CARO

GEN

(Caro and Gen are a couple. They have been together
since they were thirty-five. Caro was married before.
Gen has always been out.)

ALASTAIR

DIANA

(Alastair and Diana are lovers. They meet in a flat
they both rent for the purpose.)

JANE

(Jane is single, dates online.)

SALIM

(Salim is a recent widower. His wife
never wanted children.)

SUSAN PETERS is a GP

MOIRA is a nurse and works with Dr Peters

TIM is a speech therapist and works with Dr Peters

BENEDICT is a vicar

PAMELA arranges the church flowers

GLORIA is a cleaner

Setting:
One London street, various houses and flats.
There is a church and a Doctor's surgery.

Styles:
Narration
Scenes
Monologue
Choreography
Choral work

The Choir:
Fluctuates in size. The words here are suggestions:
further developments to be done in
collaboration with the cast.

The Word was first performed in the GBS Theatre at RADA on Friday 16 December 2016.

DIRECTOR – Vivian Munn
WRITER – Nell Leyshon
DESIGNER – Alison Neighbour
SINGING TUTOR – Philip Raymond
MOVEMENT TUTOR – Angela Gasparetto
VOICE TUTOR – Caroline Kilpatrick
SUPPORT TUTOR – Ingrid Schiller

Cast
EVA – Ana Carrigan
PETER – Jim Mulligan
JUNE – Tisa Bateman
ROBIN – Teddy Goldstein
CARO – Geraldine Stewart
GEN – Diana Hudson
ALASTAIR – James Banerjee
DIANA – Norma Wilshaw
JANE – Marsha Myers
SALIM – Mario El Mahjoub
SUSAN PETERS GP – Hilary Hodsman
MOIRA – Jeanie Deane
TIM – Richard Russell
BENEDICT – Nigel Roberts
PAMELA – Julie Davies
GLORIA – Ruth Holleley

Production Team
STAGE MANAGER – Emily Melville-Brown
DEPUTY STAGE MANAGER – Emma Dymott
ASSISTANT STAGE MANAGER – Kelly Rosser
LIGHTING DESIGNER & OPERATOR – Ariane Nixon
SOUND DESIGNER & OPERATOR – Candice Weaver
COSTUME SUPERVISOR – Sabia Smith
DESIGN ASSISTANT – Kimmy Hanseo

Day One

The CHOIR sing.

GLORIA enters alone, sweeps. She stops, looks around, addresses the audience.

GLORIA: South London. A residential street. Houses, some divided into flats. A church. A doctor's surgery. No outstanding features. Nothing out of the ordinary.

What's the word for it?

Yes. Unremarkable.

I clean for most of them. They pass my number round.

'Oh you must have Gloria. She's a gem.'

But when I show up they don't believe it's me.

They say, 'Oh I thought you'd be more…'

They mean working class. They mean common.

I've been doing it ever since he died.

The CHOIR sings the song of the street:

CHOIR: *Houses, flats, trees, shrubs. A South London street.*

The VICAR steps forward.

VICAR: It all started on a Monday.

The DOCTOR steps forward.

DOCTOR: A Tuesday. It started on a Tuesday.

VICAR: I know it was a Monday. It is the day after Sunday: it is my day off.

DOCTOR: I know it was a Tuesday. I do a four-day week in the surgery. Mondays are for catching up. Getting everything ship-shape.

VICAR: I am very aware of Mondays. I get a spiritual hangover. I drop down to earth.

CHOIR: *Houses, flats, trees, shrubs. A South London street.*

The choreographed breakfast: tables are laid, chairs placed. Newspapers are folded. People stand behind their tables.

VICAR: Breakfast is the most important meal of the day. It is a moment to break your fast, to warn your stomach that the day has begun.

DOCTOR: The body really is a most extraordinary thing. When we trained we had to do autopsies. It turns your stomach at first but you get used to it.

VICAR: It is a time to break bread.

DOCTOR: I pictured myself at the butcher's, jointing meat.

VICAR: We sow the seed and scatter and the good Lord ensures that rain falls and sun shines and the shoots emerge from the soil.

DOCTOR: The digestive system is a world of its own. I took some gastric acid from the stomach of a cadaver and placed it on a piece of wood. It burned right through.

GLORIA gives each breakfast table a quick inspection/polish, weaves her way through as though introducing each table.

GLORIA can see each person but they cannot see her: she is a cleaner.

PETER steps forward, takes his seat. EVA stands.

PETER: Breakfast.

EVA: Yes.

PETER: Sit down.

I said sit down.

EVA: Yes.

She doesn't.

PETER: Please. You make me uneasy standing there.

EVA : Do I?

PETER: Yes. Can you not just settle down?

EVA: No.

PETER: What is wrong?

EVA: A lot of things. This. All this.

PETER: All what? Go on. Say it. You always do this. You don't quite say what you mean.

Go on.

Just say it. If you have something to say just get the words out.

SALIM sits at his table. He sings 'Fly Me to the Moon' to himself. GLORIA listens.

JUNE sits down on one side of their table: ROBIN stands.

ROBIN: That is my seat.

JUNE: Where does it say that?

ROBIN: I have sat there every single day for two years.

JUNE: You haven't.

ROBIN: I have.

JUNE: We were in Venice for two weeks.

ROBIN: You know what I mean. It is my seat. I sat there two years ago and set a precedent.

JUNE: You sat with your back to the window in Venice.

ROBIN: You know why.

The buildings are shabby. They need a lot of work. And St Mark's Square…

JUNE: Is beautiful.

ROBIN: Isn't even a square.

JUNE: I can see the whole street from here. I can see.

ROBIN: It's mine. Mine. You can't just one day decide to change it.

JUNE: Why not?

ROBIN: Because I am accustomed to sitting here. I like to see out. I like my back to the wall. You can see the whole room from here, so if someone comes to attack me, I'm prepared.

CARO and GEN walk around their table. They are playing musical chairs, singing. They get faster, both sit on the same chair, laugh, then separate.

DIANA sits down. She takes a mirror from her bag, checks herself. She makes herself perfect: face, hair, clothes. She waits. ALASTAIR enters, she jumps up. They kiss.

DIANA: I thought…

ALASTAIR: I know what you thought.

DIANA: You always do. You dive right down into my mind.

They sit down.

ALASTAIR: I brought you this.

He hands her some marmalade.

DIANA: Home-made?

By your wife? Alastair? Your wife made it, didn't she?

ALASTAIR: She is very good at it. Very good.

DIANA: But she is your wife…

ALASTAIR: She doesn't know any of this. Her eyes don't see us, her heart can't bleed.

Lipstick. First thing in the morning.

Let me wipe it off.

He kisses her to silence her.

JANE enters, sits at her table. She folds her newspaper fastidiously, folds it again. She does the soduko.

JANE: Nine. Nine.

Three. Or two.

Nine. Ah. So that's three.

PETER has two newspapers, hands one to EVA, keeps one. He gives her a pen.

GLORIA: Eva. Peter.

She is not a good housekeeper. The tea towels don't get changed. The floor's never swept, I know because I put the dustpan and brush away carefully and they're in the same position the next time I come.

But she makes me tea. And she asks me how I am.

It all begins with her.

It all begins with a crossword.

PETER: Sit down.

I said sit down.

EVA: Yes.

She doesn't.

PETER: For God's sake sit down. Do the crossword.

EVA: Why?

PETER: Why what?

EVA: Why do we do them?

PETER: What?

EVA: These things. These. Is it because it makes order from chaos? Or is it because we have to do something to fill in the time before we die?

PETER: What's the matter with you?

EVA: It's true. Time is changing. It's moving in a different manner.

PETER: What are you waffling about?

EVA: I don't waffle.

PETER: Then what are you trying to say?

EVA: Nothing. Nothing at all.

One across. Entrance to a field. Four letters.

Only the answer… the answer… it eludes me.

PETER stares.

GLORIA: June. She follows me around. Commenting on the state of her own house. Middle-class guilt.

It's very tiresome.

JUNE can see EVA through her window.

ROBIN: What are you doing?

JUNE: Her. She's just standing there.

ROBIN: I can't see.

JUNE: But what's she doing?

ROBIN: Probably having breakfast.

JUNE: She isn't.

ROBIN: Breakfast starts the digestive system. It kick-starts the metabolic system.

JUNE: She doesn't normally do that.

ROBIN: What?

JUNE: Stand like that. Look.

ROBIN: I can't see. I am looking at the wall.

JUNE: The way she stands. The way she looks. Something's wrong.

EVA: Four letters. Entrance to a field.

GLORIA walks around CARO and GEN.

GLORIA: Caro. Gen. Gen. Caro.

I think they were wary at first. Thought I'd judge. She *(gestures to CARO)* has children. I've seen photos. They were in an album I was dusting. It happened to fall open at that page.

GEN: What do you fancy, scrambled or poached?

CARO: Boiled.

GEN: Soft?

CARO: Soft.

GEN: I wonder who discovered we could eat them.

CARO: What?

GEN: Well they don't look appealing. You wouldn't pick one up and say let's crack this open, see if we can eat it.

CARO: I s'pose not.

Don't foxes eat them?

GEN: Maybe people saw them eating them. Then they tried them.

Did you know that the yolk and the albumen have different nutritional qualities? Combined they are perfect food. Albumen. I like that word.

CARO: What is it in Spanish?

GEN: Albumen.

EVA: The word escapes me.

EVA folds the paper, gives up.

Look.

The sun is... The sun is...

Peter. What is it that thing the sun does?

GLORIA gestures at SALIM.

GLORIA: Number eleven. I've done all his washing and ironing since she died. He had a lot of cards. Lined the whole mantelpiece.

I dusted round all of them. Then one day he took them down. Left them on his desk. Then one day they were in the drawer and he'd signed up for online dating.

He has his first date tomorrow.

He said it to me. Directly. Said why do you do this job?

I told him the truth. I said it saved my life.

DIANA: The thing about an affair is…

ALASTAIR: … that you are never alone and you…

DIANA: … have someone with you in your mind…

ALASTAIR: … all the time.

DIANA: Very good. Again?

The thing about an affair is…

ALASTAIR: … you have a secret…

DIANA: … and no one knows and when you…

ALASTAIR: … walk around you think…

DIANA: … about it all the time.

ALASTAIR: And secrets are…

DIANA: … exciting.

GLORIA: They think they're clever. They think they have it all sorted. But everyone leaves clues.

I change their sheets. I know… everything.

GLORIA gestures at JANE.

Number nineteen. Once a fortnight, just two hours. No need for it, don't know why she bothers. It's spotless.

EVA: Entrance to a field. Entrance to a field.

PETER: What is wrong with you?

EVA: They've changed the person who sets the crossword.

PETER: Let me see.

No. It's the same.

EVA: There's a ball of yellow in the sky. Looks like an egg yolk. What is it called?

PETER: The sun?

EVA: And that thing it does when it's being the sun. When it's visible. When its rays touch us and throw our shadows on the ground?

PETER: It shines.

EVA: What shines?

PETER: Stop it. Stop it.

EVA: I don't think I… I don't think I…

JUNE: There's something wrong. Her body language. She's worried. Something's happened.

ROBIN: Stop looking at her.

It's none of your business.

CARO: Soldiers.

GEN: With butter.

CARO: Cold toast. Cold butter. No melting.

GEN: Hot. Butter dripping through.

Look at them. No net curtains, it's so blatant.

They're gawping.

CARO: What's gawping in Spanish?

GEN: There isn't the equivalent. It's a much smaller language. English swallowed other languages. It grew and grew and it's taking over.

SALIM: *(Practising.)* Hello. My name is Salim. What music do you like? The sun is very warm at the moment. Do you drink wine? Or would you prefer a cocktail?

JANE: *(Practising.)* My name is Jane. Plain Jane. No. Don't say that. My name is Jane. It's lovely to meet you.

ALASTAIR: Bring your chair round here. Closer. That's it. I want to touch you.

DIANA: Inseparable.

ALASTAIR : Siamese…

DIANA: … twins.

ALASTAIR: We are…

DIANA: … conjoined.

PETER: Eva. I think you should go to the doctor.

EVA: Why on earth would I…?

PETER: Do that?

EVA: There's… nothing wrong.

PETER: There is. You have symptoms. There must be a cause.

EVA: I'm fine. Don't fuss. You know… can't bear… fuss.

PETER: There's something wrong.

EVA: I just need some air. That's all.

She leaves the house and stands outside.

JUNE follows.

JUNE: Good morning.

EVA: Oh. Hello.

JUNE: I live in there. Number eight.

EVA: Of course.

JUNE: Are you all right? Sorry. I don't mean to interfere.

EVA: Uh, I am…

JUNE: You don't seem yourself.

EVA: Oh. Who do I seem like?

JUNE: No I mean you seem to be not quite right.

EVA: Oh I see. Well I was just trying to remember…
a thing… no.

Did you want anything else while you are here? Any
cashback? Mobile phone top-ups? Stamps?

JUNE: There's something wrong, isn't there?

EVA: Normal service will be resumed as soon as possible.

JUNE: What?

Tell me, what's wrong. What is it?

EVA: I… I… I…

*GLORIA sweeps and starts to sing. The CHOIR slowly joins till they
are all singing.*

Night.

Day Two

The following day. The sun rises. The CHOIR herald the day. Church music.

GLORIA: I clean the church as well. That's how it started.

I'd been married for twenty-five years and then one morning I woke and he was there, but he wasn't breathing. He'd gone.

After I couldn't stand the silence in the house. I went away for a while. When I moved here I put my name on the church rota to polish pews and found I liked it. I could lose myself in it.

I like to get here early. Watch the sun rise. It comes up through the stained glass. Through the red glass there.

CHOIR: *The sun sets, the moon rises.*
The moon sets, the sun rises.

Breakfast choreography. GLORIA hands out props.

PETER: I am taking you to see the doctor.

EVA: Why?

PETER: When a function is lost you can't ignore it. You have to do something.

We're going as soon as we've had breakfast.

EVA: I don't understand.

PETER: Don't be obtuse.

EVA: I can't go.

PETER: Why?

EVA: I don't have one of those... things.

PETER: You mean an appointment.

EVA: Yes.

PETER: I made you one.

EVA: But there is nothing… There is nothing…

PETER: Wrong?

EVA: Yes. Wrong. Nothing there is wrong with me.

PETER: But there is. You know there is.

ROBIN sits in the chair facing the window. JUNE stands by him.

ROBIN: Sit down.

JUNE: No. I want to keep an eye on her.

ROBIN: I'm sure she's fine. You're not responsible for the whole street.

JUNE: When I saw her yesterday, she said… she said something very…

ROBIN: What?

JUNE: She said something very… very…

ROBIN: What is it? June? What's wrong?

JUNE: I don't… I don't…

SALIM: *(Practising.)* Hello. It's so lovely to meet you.

Hello. Lovely to meet.

Kiss. Two kisses. No. Nose crash.

Handshake. Too formal.

Hello. It's so lovely to meet you.

CARO: Can we go for a walk?

GEN: No.

I need to start work.

CARO: Not now. Later. Please.

GEN: I've got to hit my target.

CARO: I hate walking on my own. I hate it when I have no one to talk to.

GEN: Then think.

CARO: I hate thinking.

GEN: I have to do four thousand words a day.

Then I need to go over it, start polishing.

CARO: It's just a translation.

GEN: It's my job. Not just that. It's a sharing of knowledge. It's making the world bigger.

JANE: *(Practising.)* Hi. Lovely to meet you. My name is Jane. I work in the library. In a world of screens, the touch of a human hand on the organisation of information is a dying craft.

So yes I am a librarian, but I try not to be a cliché.

In fact do you know where the term cliché comes from? When all printing was done by hand, letter by letter, typesetters had to keep setting the same phrases as people used them a lot. To save time they made little blocks of those phrases so they could just pick them up in one. They gave them a name. Cliché blocks.

We can be interesting, we librarians.

Too much? Too defensive?

ALASTAIR: How long do you think we can...

DIANA: … keep this up? Are you trying to…

ALASTAIR: … no no no. I just want to talk about it. I like it.

DIANA: If we talk about it I have to face what we're doing. Please. Let's just carry on.

This gets me through my days.

When I'm not with you I put on make-up, smile, but underneath, inside here, I am thinking only of you.

Say nothing.

Please. Say nothing.

End of breakfast choreography.

GLORIA: The stained glass has deep colours. It's very old. Very blue very green very yellow. The red glass is like blood and when the sun comes through it shines red on the white wall.

VICAR enters the church. PAMELA approaches with flowers.

PAMELA: They're all dying.

VICAR: Whoah. Good morning, Pamela. Lovely to see you, to hear your cheerful news.

Oh, good morning, Vicar. And how are you?

PAMELA: Good morning, Vicar.

VICAR: That's better.

PAMELA: They're all dying.

VICAR: They look fine.

PAMELA: I need to replace them.

VICAR: They can do another few days.

164

PAMELA: As soon as you cut a flower it starts to die. Slimy stems, wilted petals.

I can't stand it.

Fresh flowers every week. Bleached receptacles. That is my offering.

DOCTOR PETERS enters, flanked by MOIRA and TIM.

DOCTOR: Good morning.

MOIRA: Good morning.

TIM: Morning.

DOCTOR: No good?

TIM: Good, yes. *Good* morning.

DOCTOR: That's better. What does today promise?

TIM: The diary's full.

MOIRA: Your stethoscope is on your desk.

DOCTOR: Tongue suppressor sticks?

TIM: There's a new box. Unopened.

DOCTOR: Gloves?

MOIRA: A new box.

DOCTOR: Sharps?

MOIRA: All there.

DOCTOR: Good. Good.

Right. Let us brace ourselves. And begin.

EVA enters.

Hello. Please, come in. Have a seat.

EVA: There isn't one.

DOCTOR: Ship-shape. Come on.

TIM grabs a chair. EVA sits.

TIM and MOIRA back away.

Well?

EVA: It wasn't my idea to come.

DOCTOR: Oh. Whose idea was it?

EVA: My... My...

The big person in my house. Different from me.
I'm a... he's a...

DOCTOR: Man?

EVA: Yes.

DOCTOR: Your husband?

EVA: Fifty years.

DOCTOR: You've done well. I managed ten then five.

So why did your husband say you should come?

EVA: Because I...

He says they won't come...

DOCTOR: What won't come?

EVA: These things that come out of here.

Things that... mean things.

DOCTOR: Aha. Your words?

EVA: Yes. Can't get... out.

DOCTOR: Right. Any other signs?

EVA: No parking. One way street.

DOCTOR: Hmmm. Let me see. Rest your leg. That's it.

She examines her, tries her reflexes.

Relax. Let it go. That's perfect.

Smile for me.

Good.

Who is the Prime Minister?

EVA: It was him. The shit. Eton. Friends in high places.
Then he ran off and she's here now. Fancy shoes. Good
for kicking.

DOCTOR: What year is it?

EVA: 2016. December. On Christmas Eve I will be one... one
rotation older.

DOCTOR: One year older.

Do you forget other things? Do you find your phone in
the fridge?

EVA: No.

DOCTOR: I'm ruling out strokes. Ruling out dementia. Wrong
patterns. Always go from symptoms backwards to cause.
That's the ancient art of diagnosis.

We'll run a battery of tests on you, but I don't know
what it is.

EVA: So I am...

DOCTOR: A mystery. For now.

EVA: But I am...

DOCTOR: Well enough to go?

EVA: No. I am...

DOCTOR: Curable?

We'll see. Go home, see if the words come back to you.

JUNE: *(To audience.)* I met him, that man I live with, two...
two... things that happen, you know you get spring
summer autumn winter then it starts again. Yes those.
I met him... the man who I live with... two of those ago.

He'd been... before. He had another one of me before.
Not me but like me.

What is wrong with me?

Turns to ROBIN who approaches.

ROBIN: I've just seen that woman. Eva. She was coming
out of the health centre. She called me by her husband's
name. She asked if I could fly her home.

JUNE: I think I swallowed a...

ROBIN: Fly?

JUNE: Cloud.

PETER: *(To audience.)* I had to send her to the... to the...
person who listens to your chest, says what is wrong, finds
your... bits that aren't right.

Fifty years we have been married, shared bed... fifty...
those things... come round and round and round...
but all that time she doesn't... say... she doesn't... say.
Mysterious... there is something unknowable.

Many years. Never says...

What is it? Now I...

Now I…

What is wrong with me?

GEN: She keeps standing outside. In her front garden. She looks lost.

CARO: She can't be lost. It's her house.

GEN: I don't mean geographically. I mean in a more fundamental way. In an existential way.

CARO: I haven't eaten yet and you've used the word existential.

GEN: It's just a word, a tool of my trade.

I wonder if I should go and see her.

CARO: I thought you had work to do.

GEN: I do. But I keep thinking about this woman I read about. Her bank card ran out and her bills weren't paid. Eventually it triggered bankruptcy and when the bailiffs arrived they found her. On the floor. Dead. She had been there for five years.

CARO: This woman is alive.

GEN: We live in a community. People should speak to each other. Look out for each other.

CARO: Some people want to be alone.

GEN: We are always alone ultimately. No woman is an island and all that. You're born alone and die alone.

CARO: You're not born alone. You're born with your mother there.

GEN: You know what I mean. You can be so literal sometimes.

CARO: You tell me to be accurate. 'Each word is anchored
securely to its definition,' you say. So I try to be accurate.
Then you tell me I'm wrong again. I can't do anything right.

GEN: Maybe this afternoon I'll go and see her. After lunch.
After I've done my word count.

The street: SALIM meets ROBIN.

SALIM: Ah, Robin.

I haven't seen you for a long time.

ROBIN: No. A very long...

SALIM: ... time?

ROBIN: Time, yes. I've been meaning to call in. I wanted
to mention the grass. It's all rather long. There's seed
heads... blow about. And then before you know it you
have those... those things. Plants you don't want.

SALIM: Daffodils?

ROBIN: No.

SALIM: I don't want daffodils. Too yellow.

ROBIN: Not them, no. The others.

They're called...

They're called...

Plants come in two types. Ones you want, ones you
don't want.

SALIM stares.

They're... pernicious. They... grow where you don't
want them.

SALIM: I'm sorry. I don't know what you mean.

ROBIN: No. Categories. Categories.

SALIM: I will try to cut the grass. Since my wife died, it's been hard to keep up but I will do it. This weekend.

Robin, can I ask you a question?

This shirt. What do you think? Is it flattering?

ROBIN: It makes you look very... not old... opposite of old?

SALIM: Young.

ROBIN: You look like a spring... a spring... peacock.

SALIM: Are you all right?

ROBIN: This thing... The woman in my house has a thing...

SALIM: What thing?

ROBIN: I don't know.

I don't know.

ROBIN leaves. SALIM checks his shirt, his hair.

DIANA and ALASTAIR approach. They are surprised to see SALIM. DIANA pulls back, but it is too late.

SALIM: Good morning.

DIANA: Hello, Salim.

This is... *(She searches for a name and fails.)* Alastair. He came round to give me some advice.

ALASTAIR: *(Quick.)* She's thinking of moving.

SALIM: Aha. Estate agent. You can tell by the suit. The only ones who dress up. You go to the theatre they're in jeans, you go to the races they're in jeans.

DIANA: Not the jockeys.

SALIM: Ha ha. No.

That's a shame you're thinking of moving. Is it worth much?

ALASTAIR: More than yesterday, less than tomorrow. That's London for you. It's a bubble. But there've always been bubbles.

DIANA: Sorry I don't mean to be rude but we need to get going. I have a lot to do.

ALASTAIR: South sea bubble. Tulip bubble. It's hysteria really, basic human behaviour. A fear of missing out. We are pack animals. Look at sheep. Once one panics, they all go.

DIANA: Not me.

ALASTAIR: She's a lone wolf.

DIANA: Thank you for coming to see the house.

ALASTAIR: My pleasure. It was a most enjoyable experience. I think it'll sell easily.

SALIM: Can I ask you both something? I'm trying to look at how I dress. I want to know… I mean it's very… nice quality. Where did you get your… this…

ALASTAIR: My suit?

SALIM: Yes. Was it off the… off the…

ALASTAIR: Peg? Lord no. I had it made.

DIANA: We must go. Time is marching on.

SALIM: Soldiers.

DIANA: Sorry?

SALIM: Marching. Marauding.

DIANA: Are you all right?

SALIM: I can't... Yes... No... I keep...

GLORIA moves them all back in line.

The VICAR steps forward.

VICAR: It's hard not to think of them as your flock. The parish has boundaries, sort of like the walls. You know like dry stone walls keeping the sheep in.

People move in and out. Fresh blood.

Our numbers are falling.

PAMELA: The vase has disappeared again.

VICAR: Good morning, Pamela.

PAMELA: Good morning, Vicar.

VICAR: That's better.

PAMELA: Someone has been in and stolen it all.

VICAR: I put it in the cupboard.

PAMELA: And the bleach? I can't find it.

VICAR: You used it all. I don't think there's any need to use quite so much.

PAMELA: Germs.

VICAR: But the smell.

PAMELA: The smell of rotting stems.

VICAR: It catches in the throat.

PAMELA: Dirty slimy stems. Rotting.

VICAR: A natural process.

PAMELA: It might be God's work but it stinks.

DOCTOR : *(To audience.)* We have a team at the surgery. I have a speech therapist.

TIM steps forward.

A nurse.

MOIRA steps forward.

They are worth their weight in gold.

TIM: We just do our job.

MOIRA: We deliver the services which are needed.

TIM: Which are vital.

DOCTOR: Working here leaves you open to contagious disease. People walk in, cough all over you. Your immune system grows in strength. Mine is like a Russian tank.

VICAR: You ask me about my immune system? It is looked after. It is taken care of. Prayer is a very very powerful tool.

TIM: Communication. Words.

To speak is to transfer the contents of one mind to another mind.

It is a form of magic. The words are spells.

There are two elements to speech. Yes, two.

The first is the physical. To speak is a complex and subtle action. Muscles and breath are coordinated. There is pitch. Tone.

The second is the content. The what to say, where the desire to speak comes from. The inner world. The spiritual, if you like.

To communicate is vital. Nearly twenty percent of adults have had communication difficulties at one point in their lives. More than half of prisoners have problems communicating.

I try to work on both elements. Physical and content. People need their voices.

NURSE: For the more intimate examinations I act as a chaperone. It protects the doctor, protects the patient, protects all of us. Protection is a very important thing. We need to be protected from being accused of inappropriate behaviour, from being sued, and of course, from catching whatever they have brought in.

EVA approaches.

DOCTOR: I think it's a virus. Nothing else shows up.

EVA: How does it... how did I...? Do they do that thing? Lift off the ground, go in the...

DOCTOR: Probably airborn, yes.

EVA: Creatures, not visible.

DOCTOR: We think it's passed on by talking. Or touching. Or just being in close proximity.

EVA: Will... will... *(Points at the DOCTOR.)*

DOCTOR: I don't think so. Not a lot gets through.

EVA: I... er...

DOCTOR: So we need to think about what to do next.

EVA: I... I...

DOCTOR: The problem is we don't know what we're dealing with. I'd like to do some more tests. We'll take blood, saliva, any other bodily fluids you might have hanging around. I'd like you to come back tomorrow.

EVA turns, meets GEN.

GEN: Hi.

EVA: Oh... er... don't come too...

GEN: I thought I'd introduce myself. I live here. It occurred to me that we live on the same street and we've never actually spoken.

EVA: I... don't...

GEN: I'm Genevieve. Gen.

I work from home. I'm a translator. Of books.

Sorry I don't even know your name.

EVA: I... I...

GEN: Are you all right?

EVA: Things swim along.

GEN: You mean on the canal?

EVA: Long... boats pulled by those things.

GEN: Engines?

EVA: Four legs. Stuff on top of their skin. *(Demonstrates.)* Ears. *(Neighs.)*

GEN: Horses?

EVA: I... sorry. Your name?

GEN: Gen.

Are you all right?

EVA: Never been…

GEN: Better?

> Look if there's ever anything you need, I'd like to think you could come round and ask for it.

> I'm just here.

TIM: *(To audience.)* Two elements. First, the physical. We need to work on the muscles of the mouth and throat. Build up exercises which warm and strengthen.

> La la la.

> And then we build up to more sophisticated exercises. Sound repetitions, and eventually, phrases which we repeat.

> The wily red fox jumped over the horse.

CHOIR: *The wily red fox jumped over the horse.*

DIANA: I liked you as the…

ALASTAIR: … the man in the suit who…

DIANA: … estate…

ALASTAIR: … man who…

DIANA: … says how…

ALASTAIR: … much money the…

DIANA: Can we do it again? Can we play… can we be… different from what we…

ALASTAIR: The time. I am supposed to go… back to the thing I live with… to the…

DIANA: Thing in your house?

ALASTAIR: Made the marma–

DIANA: –lade. The sun is in the fridge.

ALASTAIR: Gold.

DIANA: Butter.

ALASTAIR: Yes.

DIANA: What are we…

ALASTAIR: Yes what are we?

DIANA: I think we are… lost.

GLORIA: He saw me cleaning the church and asked if I wanted to work for him. In the vicarage. Next door.

He didn't know anything of my story, of what had happened.

He started passing my number on to do me a favour. Word of mouth. Recommendation.

He's a clean man. Bible by the bedside. Frocks in the cupboard. Cleanliness and godliness.

Oh, I know everything.

GEN approaches CARO.

CARO: Ah, it's the neighbourhood watch.

GEN: I just said hello. That's… all.

CARO: I used to like the way you spoke to everyone. Now I'm not sure.

GEN: You don't want to… you… what is the thing when other people have a piece.

CARO: Share?

GEN: Yes you have shares in me.

CARO: What?

GEN: Shareholder. Sharecropper. Plowshare.

CARO: Gen? Are you all right?

GEN: Yes.

CARO: You're not making sense. What is it?

GEN: I don't…

CARO: You don't know.

GEN: No.

> *JANE enters. She waits.*
>
> *SALIM enters.*

JANE: Hello.

SALIM: Er… Jane?

JANE: Yes. You are Salim?

You live in my street.

SALIM: Yes.

JANE: Oh that's, what is it? Well it's funny, isn't it?

I mean we've never spoken but I've seen you, of course I have.

> *SALIM steps forward, forgets whether he was going to kiss her. He is awkward, loses his way, holds out his hand. He has forgotten what he planned to say.*

SALIM: I… I…

It's lovely to… are you… have you eaten?

JANE: Am I hungry? Not really, I have the appetite of a bird.

SALIM: An eagle?

JANE: No. That's funny.

SALIM: Is it?

JANE: Yes. I don't eat roadkill. I don't rip the flesh from bones.

SALIM: A... a... glass of...?

JANE: That would be lovely.

SALIM: White? The one with bubbles? Or the other one?

JANE: Red?

SALIM: That's it. Two.

> *They are handed glasses. They clink.*

Er... Sal... chee...

JANE: Cheers.

> I know your story. I'm sorry. About your wife. It must be so hard.

SALIM: Thank you. It was... yes. But I'm... ready.

JANE: Ready for?

SALIM: For this. You know, to meet people and... *(Holds up his glass.)*

JANE: Drink.

> Funny to think that when we were sending the messages, we were just a few doors away from each other. How does it work exactly? Did they bounce off a satellite? It's a lovely thought, that they came out of our houses, were beamed right up there, then bounced back, down into our street.

Imagine if you could see our words passing through the sky.

SALIM: When I was… not big… when I was a…

JANE: Child?

SALIM: I always wanted to go… up?

JANE: Where?

SALIM: To the thing up… You know. It changes shape as the… thirty or so days pass.

JANE: Twenty-eight days.

SALIM: Yes. The…

JANE: Moon. You wanted to go to the moon?

SALIM: Do you think I'll ever get there?

JANE: I don't know.

(Sings.) Fly me to the moon…

SALIM: *Let me fly among the…*

JANE: … *stars.*

GLORIA: And then he gave my number to the surgery. I do it in the evening, when everyone has gone.

I empty the sharps bin. I clean everything, imagine mopping up all the germs, killing the viruses.

No virus is completely resistant.

Except life.

DOCTOR: We are facing an epidemic.

VICAR: It is a visitation.

Much of life is mysterious.

DOCTOR: The word epidemic comes from the words 'epi-demos'. Upon the people.

We will work out the cause and find a cure. That is our job. It is what we do. Symptom, cause. Problem, solution.

VICAR: We know nothing of all this. We know nothing. However, there is a presence which knows everything.

There is a design behind all of this. Behind all that happens.

CHOIR: *Epidemic*
Virus
Germs
Mystery
Visitation
Design

Sunset. The day ends.

Night.

Day Three

Everyone in the street now has the virus.

The day begins with GLORIA cleaning.

GLORIA: *(To audience.)* It took me a long time to get back any sense of joy, of wonder.

It was a shock to be on my own. To do what I wanted.

I started by going out at night. Into the garden. With the plants. Atropa Belladonna.

Atropos held the shears which could cut the thread of life.

Belladonna. Beautiful woman.

I didn't mean to do it.

I didn't mean it.

So the garden. Yes I came out into the garden. I used to watch the sun set. Watch the moon rise.

It's a small miracle really. It happens every night without fail.

Breakfast choreography while singing distorted and confused lyrics:

CHOIR: *Fly me to the silver*
Let me... among the stars
Let me see what after winter before summer the time
When the yellow flowers come out
On a Jupiter and a Mars.

PETER: You... did you want to... say?

EVA: In here...

I have…

… things.

PETER: You want? *(He passes the newspaper.)*

EVA: I can't…

In here…

PETER: Spit it… Get them… ar-tic-u-late.

EVA: Things for me…

Inside…

Need to get them…

Need… need… need… need…

Voice…

Voice…

GEN : You are my…

CARO: I am…

GEN: You are my…

Words… floating… They used to have…

CARO: Weight?

GEN: Those things plants have, the bit that goes down that sucks up water and… other stuff which makes it… bigger.

CARO: Feathers?

SALIM and JANE sit on their separate tables but they can see each other.

SALIM: What about going for a… not tea. The other one.

JANE: A thing that holds… liquid.

SALIM takes money from his pocket.

SALIM: I've got some... let me...

JANE: How many?

He shows her his money.

SALIM: One... two... eight... five...

JANE: One... five... two...

SALIM: Folding ones. Metal circles.

They have... numbers. You can change them for...

JANE: Things.

SALIM: Yes. Things.

DIANA: This can't...

Do you think all of this is...

Punish–

ALASTAIR: –ment.

DIANA: Punishment. To stop us...

ALASTAIR: ... whispering sweet...

DIANA: ... somethings.

ALASTAIR: This is...

DIANA: ... bad.

ALASTAIR: Love.

DIANA: Up there someone...

ALASTAIR: ... isn't...

DIANA: ... sees me, knows.

ALASTAIR: Watching.

DIANA holds up her hand, shows her wedding ring.

DIANA: Gold.

ALASTAIR: Trap.

DIANA: Circle.

ALASTAIR: Shackle.

DIANA: Sign.

ROBIN: I say.

JUNE: Yes.

ROBIN: You look…

JUNE: I?

ROBIN: Window.

Is she?

JUNE: There. That thing outside. Not short. Hair has colour drained from it.

She is a… she is a…

ROBIN: Is there blood going round, heart… pumping…

JUNE: Yes.

ROBIN: Skin holding it together, keeping the organs from…

JUNE: From spilling?

ROBIN: Spilling. All that holds us… thin layer.

Could this…

Could this…

I am… empty.

JUNE: Woman.

ROBIN: *(Pointing at her chair.)* You are in my… Wall. Eyes.
Can't.

JUNE: Food. I want food.

ROBIN: I want I want I want.

I am… empty.

GEN: Look.

CARO: Today… what are we…

GEN: Work.

CARO: Those… things…

GEN: Pages of the things… those things…

Small black things…

CARO: … white pages.

GEN: Things we…

CARO: Say.

GEN: Read. These… coming out of my… mouth.

DIANA: Words.

ALASTAIR: Yes.

DIANA: This can't…

ALASTAIR: No.

DIANA: … continue.

Stop. We need to…

ALASTAIR: Stop?

SALIM stands, walks towards JANE.

SALIM: Are you?

JANE: Not.

SALIM: I am…

JANE: Don't…

SALIME: What to…?

JANE: Can't… They won't…

SALIM: With me?

JANE: I… I…

SALIM: Oh.

JANE: I…

SALIM leaves even though JANE wants him to stay.

PETER: What do you…?

EVA: What?

Fifty years.

PETER: Same bed.

EVA: You.

PETER: Me.

EVA: And me.

PETER: Waffle.

EVA: No.

PETER: Always like this. Since then.

EVA: No.

PETER: Don't understand…

Now. Listen. Mind has facts.

EVA: No.

PETER: Engineered.

EVA: No.

PETER: Simple.

EVA: No.

PETER: Facts.

EVA: *(Shouts.)* No.

Silence.

PETER: I know you.

EVA: Trying to…

Other way…

PETER: One-way street.

EVA: Cul-de-sac.

In here.

All in here.

Secrets. Can't get…

Inside.

Secrets.

CHOIR sing a word scramble of the epidemic, a bursting through in sound. They include words from all of them:

CHOIR: *Feathers*
  Gold
  Shackles
  Circles
  Food
  Plant
  Flowers

DOCTOR: The natural order is disturbed.

VICAR: The natural order is designed.

DOCTOR: What they really seek is for all to return to normal. For all to be shipshape.

VICAR: We have no power. In the face of all of this we have nothing.

DOCTOR: They seek a cure. We seek a cure.

VICAR: The act of getting onto your knees brings us down to the earth.

DOCTOR: We survive illnesses every day which would once have killed us.

A broken nail, the infection sets in, the blood is poisoned. Bang. Six feet below the ground.

An appendix. Bang. Ashes to ashes.

Measles. Bang. Dust to dust.

Pneumonia, the old man's friend. Bang. Gone.

VICAR: Prayer. Faith.

DOCTOR: Antibiotics were a marvellous discovery. We need to look for a cure, for treatment, for recovery.

She turns to TIM.

Rehab.

She turns to the NURSE.

Rehab.

TIM: The physical element alone will not cure.

We need to work on the second element. The content. The what to say, the desire to speak. The inner world. The spiritual, if you like.

MOIRA: They need reassurance. We all do.

TIM: Oh yes. A lot of the reluctance to speak is psychological. Words are trapped inside. The boundary between the external world and the internal world is restrictive.

To express what we feel inside us is a powerful act.

To repress and contain what we feel inside us is a violent act.

MOIRA: I tend to touch them.

I find it helps.

TIM: I like to begin with exercises to warm the voice, to loosen the muscles we use.

La la la la. Stretch your mouth. La la la la. Open further. Now smaller.

CHOIR: *La la la la.*
La la la la.

MOIRA: Every appointment I make it a mission to apply touch.

TIM: We need to work on the larynx. A tight throat never speaks words.

Massage it. La la la.

MOIRA: Touch reassures. It is a connection – a nonverbal connection – between people.

I'm aware of my hands. I look after them.

I put cream on them every night. When I am doing the gardening I wear protective gloves.

My hands, these two hands, have touched many people. They have held a girl's hand while she received an injection.

They have cut and removed stitches one by one from a builder's coarse palm. He cried.

They have held the hands of a woman who lost her baby. I cried.

The touch of human skin on human skin is very very powerful.

VICAR: Hands together. Human skin on human skin.

Prayer. Faith.

He turns to PAMELA.

We need flowers. Incense. The prayer book.

PAMELA: It is all there.

VICAR: We need to sing.

PAMELA: We can.

The wood's polished. The floor swept.

VICAR: When did you do that?

PAMELA: Last night.

It was dark and I didn't put the lights on. Just a couple of candles.

I like it that way, always like to be alone.

I could hear your singing. I could hear the choir.

CHOIR begins singing sacred music.

EVA approaches.

VICAR: You don't have to speak. You only need to tell me what you wish to be absolved of.

Guilt is a heavy burden.

EVA: I have…

Not that.

VICAR: Secrets? They corrupt.

EVA: This…

VICAR: Honesty is purity. Honesty is cleanliness.

EVA: Inside there is…

VICAR: Go on.

EVA: …someone…

VICAR: Yes?

EVA: Diff…

VICAR: Difficult?

EVA: No.

VICAR: Diffident?

EVA: No!

VICAR: Different?

EVA: That one.

Can't…

Can't…

VICAR: Let us begin again. In the beginning…

EVA: It all started with a cross…

VICAR: Yes he was crucified on a cross.

EVA: No.

VICAR: He was. There is evidence.

EVA: This started…

VICAR: It started in a garden.

EVA: Epidemic. Started with a cross word.

VICAR: What?

EVA: The things not coming.

VICAR: Your words?

EVA: Need new… need new…

Need…

VICAR: Shall we pray? Prayer delivers us what we need. We pray for the return of the word.

EVA: I want to… I want to…

Without them I am…

This. Only this.

I need new…

PETER enters.

PETER: You look…

He takes her arm, leads her from the church.

The CHOIR changes; the music becomes secular.

EVA: Something…

PETER: You need…

EVA: I need…

PETER: … to stop.

EVA: To start. To start. To start.

They are with the DOCTOR.

DOCTOR: How are you?

PETER: We are…

EVA: I…

PETER: We are…

DOCTOR: Let's try something. We don't know if it will work but we can observe you. There will be measurable outcomes.

Take these every hour. With milk.

And this.

TIM steps forward.

TIM: I have an exercise sheet for you. First thing, last thing.

You'll need to exercise your throat, larynx, tonsils, tongue, facial muscles.

MOIRA: Here. Hold my hand.

TIM: And then think about what you want to say.

MOIRA: Your skin is dry.

TIM: Think about why you are going to speak.

MOIRA: You will be fine.

TIM: Where the impulse comes from.

DOCTOR: Modern medicine targets like a missile. It locks on. Destroys.

VICAR: You need to pray. Believe in your body's ability to cure itself.

DOCTOR: Take your medicine.

VICAR: Have faith.

DOCTOR: Symptoms. Cause. Cure.

VICAR: Belief can cure.

DOCTOR: Elimination.

VICAR: Faith.

EVA: I need to think.

I need to…

I need…

I…

They all fall away and EVA is alone. The CHOIR interweaves secular and spiritual.

It builds to a climax.

Night falls.

It is dark. Silent.

Day Four

The sun rises.

GLORIA enters.

Breakfast choreography in silence.

The ten people who are affected by the epidemic eat, argue over chairs, over who can see out of the window.

All communication is through gesture and takes on some elements of the breakfast choreography.

The day is carried out in silence. And then, when she is happy with the day, GLORIA steps forward.

GLORIA: Atropa Belladonna. Deadly nightshade.

I didn't mean to do it.

His pupils were so small his eyes were the colour of the leaves of the plant.

I resettled. Moved. After prison it was the light that surprised. It hurt my eyes, made my pupils like his, so I looked like he did before his heart stopped before it all stopped.

He *(gestures at the VICAR)* preaches forgiveness.

He knows nothing. They know nothing.

I know everything.

GLORIA weaves her way through. They don't hear her.

I fold her clothes.

Empty his pockets.

He smokes and wears patches. Hides the packets in his bag.

In the rubbish I found drink bottles tucked inside fruit juice cartons.

Saucepans thick with mould.

She hasn't read a page of her book in the last month.

And you. His pants are by the bed every day.

And you. Foot deodorant. Corn plasters.

And you. Knicker drawer secrets.

And you. Magazines. Old style. Under the mattress.

And you. And you. And you. And you.

GLORIA reaches EVA.

And you.

I know everything.

I know what it is to be within four walls.

Bars on the window.

EVA stands forward. Something is happening.

Come out into the garden. Yes, come out.

Come out into the garden.

Watch the sun set. Watch the moon rise.

It's a small miracle really.

It happens every night without fail.

The day ends. The light falls.

The CHOIR quietly begins, then builds.

CHOIR: *The sun sets. The moon rises.*
The moon sets. The sun rises.
Night gives way to day.
Day gives way to night.
Dark gives way to light.
Light gives way to dark.

Sun sets.

Dark comes.

Day Five

Breakfast choreography. GLORIA watches.

PETER: I…

    Are you?

    What?

EVA: Am I what? You keep opening your mouth and gaping and anyone would think you don't have words.

PETER: You…

EVA: Did you hear that?

PETER: I think…

EVA: I spoke. Properly. Words. Sentences.

    Hold on. Pass me that. Quick.

    PETER passes the newspaper, folded at the crossword page.

    Entrance to a field. Four letters. Gate.

    Entrance to a house. Four letters. Door.

    Entrance to the world. Four letters. Word.

DOCTOR: A cure can come without warning. There is a point of balance in the body when the fight is taking place. In one corner the virus's forces. In the other the cure's forces.

    It is war.

VICAR: Revelation. Epiphany. When prayers are answered things change. The world changes.

PETER: Eva.

Can I get you something? You need to eat this morning.

EVA: Listen. You did it. You too.

PETER: What did I do?

EVA: Spoke.

PETER: I did, didn't I?

EVA: Your syntax was correct. Your words fell in the right order.

You spoke and an idea was passed from your mind into my mind via the medium of language.

PETER: You sound so clear. It's not like you.

EVA: Is it not?

PETER: No.

EVA: I sound clear. Like water.

So clear. So very very clear.

DOCTOR: Some illnesses cure themselves.

MOIRA: Most do.

TIM: The vast majority of people find they can improve their speech.

DOCTOR: But we have to appear to be doing something.

MOIRA: We need to hold their hands and give them something to swallow.

TIM: Some people find an impetus. A blockage clears.

DOCTOR: If they have medicine they are cured earlier.

MOIRA: They like to clutch a prescription.

Sometimes I wish I could give them a bag of sweets.

VICAR: We don't always hear prayers being answered. Cure comes about in a mysterious manner.

PAMELA approaches. Places down fresh flowers.

EVA looks at her crossword.

EVA: Cure. Seven letters.

VICAR: Miracle.

DOCTOR: Medical.

EVA: Panacea.

EVA looks at PETER.

EVA: Talk to me.

PETER: What do you want me to say?

EVA: What do you have to say?

PETER: I sense your question is leading. I need you to tell me what you want to hear. I am an engineer. I want to fit the brief.

EVA: Listen to you, speaking like that. So clearly.

You caught it from me. You are cured by me.

If they caught it from me, I can cure them.

PETER: You think you have the power to do that?

Really?

EVA: I do, yes.

PETER: How irrational.

EVA: Is it?

It is how I feel.

EVA leaves the house, meets GEN.

EVA: *(To GEN.)* Hello. I am so sorry. When we spoke, I think I may have infected you.

GEN: I…

EVA: I don't want you to worry.

GEN: No.

EVA: You'll be fine.

GEN: My…

EVA: I can cure you. Like this. By talking.

Your words will return.

GEN turns to CARO.

EVA turns away, JUNE approaches.

EVA: June.

JUNE: I…

EVA: I can cure you. Like this. By talking.

Your words will return.

JUNE turns to ROBIN.

ROBIN turns to SALIM.

SALIM turns to JANE, EVA turns to DIANA, JUNE turns to ALASTAIR.

It is street choreography and the cure is passed, hand to hand, person to person.

Words return.

EVA: The words will come. Try.

JUNE: I am going to. Oh. I can speak. Look.

CARO: All I wanted today was eggs. Scrambled. Oh.

GEN: And I thought you meant poached. Oh.

ROBIN: Cutting grass keeps the weeds down. Weeds. Weeds. Of course. That's what I wanted to say.

SALIM: I really wanted to meet someone else. The house is too quiet. I don't want to be on my own.

JANE: I tend not to speak in clichés.

ALASTAIR: She is utterly irresistible.

DIANA: I can speak for myself.

They return to the breakfast tables.

ALASTAIR: The thing about an affair is…

DIANA: … it is essentially dishonest…

ALASTAIR: No. The thing about an affair is…

DIANA: … it always fades. Normality returns.

ALASTAIR: I thought this would be different.

DIANA: And so did I.

JANE moves over to SALIM.

JANE: Do you mind if I sit with you. Breakfast alone, it's, well it's… I am trailing off because I'm feeling a groundswell of emotion, not because I am ill.

SALIM: Please.

I like your accuracy.

JANE: I like to think of my internal world as a library. I catalogue it.

SALIM: Precision.

JANE: Yes. Exactly. I dislike muddled communication. I am a fan of clarity.

SALIM: Do you like this colour shirt?

JANE: It accentuates your eyes.

SALIM: Thank you.

I have three types of tea. Do you have a preference?

JANE: No. Please choose for me. Surprise me.

GEN: The Spanish for 'if only' is 'ojalá'.

It is so much nicer. I like the sound of it. Ojalá. It holds promise.

CARO: It has rhythm.

GEN: Yes.

CARO: A poached egg is very satisfying.

GEN: If done correctly. A drop of vinegar.

Poached then?

CARO: I think so.

Is she there?

GEN: She's fine. I can see her. She's talking. She's more... what is the word. Animated. That's it. She has a vitality she didn't have before.

ROBIN: Allow me to explain more fully.

We get a new table, a wider one. Not a square exactly, more of a rectangle, or even a rhomboid. The long side along here. We put chairs this side.

JUNE: Sit side by side? As though we are on a bus?

ROBIN: We can see each other if we turn our heads, but we can both see outside.

JUNE: Yes. I see. It sounds as though it would work.

Look. She looks different doesn't she? Incredible what one can reveal about oneself without using a single word.

ROBIN: Yes.

JUNE: Up close I think it's different as we're bombarded with information. But like this, through glass, it's like another art form. Ballet or dance.

Words become superfluous.

PETER: You want this? *(Offers newspaper.)*

EVA: No.

PETER: No crossword?

EVA: I am bored of them.

PETER: Why? You always do it.

EVA: I'm bored of all this. Bored of everything.

PETER: Bored? You sound like a child.

EVA: That's it.

PETER: What?

EVA: I feel like a child. Like a child with new words.

I have new words for new thoughts.

PETER: What new thoughts?

EVA: You sound worried. I'm not about to run away.
Or reinvent myself. It's too late for that.

PETER: That's a relief.

EVA: I just want to make some changes.

PETER: Oh God.

EVA: Change is good.

PETER: I like it the way it is.

EVA: That is you. You are a creature of habit. You are a
Labrador. You seek the smelly blanket, the toy, the dinner
at six.

PETER: And you? What do you want?

EVA: I don't know. I haven't worked it out yet. I am going to
think about it.

PETER: What kind of thing?

EVA: I'll see. I want to use different words, a different syntax.
I want to be bold enough to speak.

PETER: What's happened? You're not like you.

EVA: I am me.

PETER: You're different.

EVA: Illness changes us.

PETER: I don't like it.

EVA: You'll survive.

PETER: I find it all most odd. All unfathomable.

EVA: I don't.

PETER: It's so mysterious.

EVA: I agree. It is a mystery. Something strange.

But I think I understand.

In some way, down inside me, down below my words, down where cold rivers run, where winds blow and clouds spill rain, where trees grow vast and green, where plants send out tendrils which choke, where mists are dried up by the morning sun, where apples decay on the ground, where birds are drunk on rotten fruit, where primates carry their young for a year, where fish leap silver out of the water, where animals snarl and tear flesh with their teeth, where it is harder to kill a plant than grow it, down there where language has never been and I do not live, down there, in that world, I think I understand.

CHOIR sing.

Choreography putting away breakfast. Clearing stage.

They leave.

GLORIA is the last on stage. She sweeps, picks up the last things. She sings. She leaves. The stage is clear.

The singing ends off stage.

Silence.

The light dies.

End.

DOWN THE HATCH
by Frances Poet

All rights whatsoever in this play are strictly reserved and application for performance etc. should be made before rehearsal to Macnaughton Lord Representation, 3 The Glass House, Royal Oak Yard, London, SE1 3GE. No performance may be given unless a licence has been obtained.

Down the Hatch was first performed in the GBS Theatre at RADA on Friday 15 December 2017.

DIRECTOR – Vivian Munn
DESIGNER – Eleanor Field
MOVEMENT DIRECTOR – Angela Gasparetto
VOICE TUTOR – Caroline Kilpatrick
SINGING TUTOR – Philip Raymond
SUPPORT TUTOR – Ingrid Schiller

Cast
ANUSHKA – Norma Wilshaw
BRENDA – Vicki Edmunds
JONATHAN – Nigel Roberts
JULIA – Ruth Holleley
JAMES – Drew Paterson
PETER – Marek Urbanowicz
MARGARET – Catherine Herman
PAM – Paulette McLatchie
ELIZABETH – Leah Hoskin
GEORGE – Jim Mulligan
OSCAR – Martin Doolan
EDWARD – Charles Molloy
THE NURSE – Tisa Bateman
GIOVANNI – Mario El Mahjoub
MORVEN – Hilary Hodsman
ROGER – Neville Price

Production Team
STAGE MANAGER – Lucy Mason-Lockett
DEPUTY STAGE MANAGER – Lauren Ione
ASSISTANT STAGE MANAGER – Zarah Cooper
LIGHTING DESIGNER & OPERATOR – Joseph Thomas
SOUND DESIGNER & OPERATOR – Aiden Connor
WARDROBE ASSISTANT – Nicola Stimpson
SCENIC ARTIST – Aidan Carroll

GATHERING

The impressive dining room of a rather grand Highland retreat.

ANUSHKA is finishing setting the table. The sound of a Polish pop song bleeds out of her headphones. She sings along, not very well but joyfully uninhibited.

BRENDA enters, a little apprehensive. ANUSHKA hasn't seen her so BRENDA, amused, watches her singing away for a while. She can't resist copying her a little, picking up the tune and imitating ANUSHKA's moves. ANUSHKA turns and sees her for the first time.

BRENDA stops abruptly. ANUSHKA gives BRENDA a scathing look and exits.

BRENDA wanders around the table. She sees something she doesn't like, tuts, picks up a silver spoon and shines it. Satisfied, she returns it to the table. Her feet are killing her. She sits down. Nobody is looking so she slips her shoes off - that's better.

JONATHAN enters.

JONATHAN: Hello.

We've met before, haven't we.

BRENDA: We have, loads of times. Hello Jonathan.

JONATHAN: I thought a place like this would have its own staff.

BRENDA: It does. Just seen one of them staging her own little indoor rave.

JONATHAN: Why have Edward and Margaret got you up here then?

BRENDA: I'm a bloody guest, just like you.

JONATHAN: Oh, I'm so sorry.

BRENDA: They better not be expecting me to clean. I've only brought my best shoes.

JONATHAN notices her shoes for the first time.

JONATHAN: Oh they're lovely. Smashing colour. And look at that heel. Very elegant.

BRENDA: Thought you worked in finance, not footwear.

JONATHAN: I just like beautiful things.

BRENDA: And yet you married Julia.

JONATHAN is too busy looking at BRENDA's shoes to pick up BRENDA's joke so she takes it further.

She's a sour little thing, ain't she? Face like she's been sucking on a quarter of Acid Drops.

JONATHAN: *(Not having listened.)* Hmmm, yes.

BRENDA: Do you want to try them on or something?

JONATHAN: Much too small for me, I'll bet. What are they? A seven?

BRENDA: Eight and a half, actually. What size are you?

JONATHAN : Eight and a half. How funny.

BRENDA: Go on, then. Try them if you want.

JONATHAN: No, I couldn't.

It's Barbara, isn't it?

BRENDA: No. Try again.

JONATHAN: It's definitely a B, your name.

BRENDA: Is it?

JONATHAN: Belinda?

She shakes her head.

Bethany?

She shakes her head.

Bryony?

BRENDA: Misery on a motorbike, seriously?

JONATHAN: Becky? Betty? Bitty?

BRENDA: That's not even a bloody name.

JONATHAN: *(All spoken in the same breath.)* Beverly, Brooke, Belle, Bea, Bridget, Blossom, Beatrix, Bernadette, Bianca, Barbi, Bambi?

BRENDA: You're just getting sillly now.

JONATHAN: Bree?

BRENDA: That's a bloody cheese, that is.

JONATHAN: Go on then, tell me.

BRENDA: Sarah.

JONATHAN: No!

BRENDA: Are you bloody twp? It's Brenda.

JONATHAN: It was a B! It was on the tip of my tongue.

BRENDA: Clearly.

JONATHAN: I might give those shoes a try, you know.

BRENDA: Whatever floats your boat.

JONATHAN takes his shoes off, quite rushed, and then, with much more care and reverence, places his feet in BRENDA's shoes. He admires them, then fairly proficiently stands up in them and takes a little turn. JULIA enters and with barely a glance at him, snaps at her husband.

JULIA: Jonathan, take those off at once.

JONATHAN does as he's told.

JULIA (CONT'D): Hello Brenda, why on earth are you here?

BRENDA: I was invited.

JULIA: Bloody hell. Daddy's gone mad. I saw Oscar walking the grounds, singing his heart out.

JONATHAN: Oscar?

JULIA: Daddy's gardener, for Christ's sake. I thought this must be some sort of late birthday celebration or an early one or I don't know, is it Daddy and Margaret's anniversary? Why didn't the invitation say? And whatever it is, why has he invited all his former staff?

BRENDA: Me and your Dad had our special moments, actually. And he used to spend hours walking round the garden with Oscar. If it was "all his former staff", Pam would be here wouldn't she?

JULIA: Who's Pam?

BRENDA: Ha! I almost wish she was here just to hear you say that. Used to tell me you and she had a special bond.

JULIA: What are you talking about?

BRENDA: She was the other cleaner. Worked for your Dad even longer than me. Irritating smile, no sense of humour, a real brown noser. Head so far up your step-mother's ass, it's not even accurate to call her an ass kisser.

JONATHAN: Friend of yours then?

BRENDA: She's no butty of mine.

JULIA: I can't picture her at all.

JAMES and PETER enter. PETER is wearing a rather garish shirt.

JAMES: Julia!

(To PETER.) You see, they're here already. I told you we wouldn't be the first.

PETER: *(Under his breath to JAMES.)* And I told you I would like a few more minutes to get ready.

JAMES: *(Under his breath to PETER.)* You'd tried on everything in the suitcase. How much longer did you need?

(Full voice to JULIA.) Darling, you look beautiful.

Goes in for a hug, JULIA, cold, proffers her cheek for a kiss.

JULIA: No, I don't.

JAMES: Jonathan!

Hugs and handshakes between the men.

JONATHAN: James. Peter. Good to see you.

JULIA: Peter.

Without much thought, JAMES puts out his hand to introduce himself to BRENDA.

JAMES: Hello I'm/ (James)

BRENDA: I know who you are, James. I knew you were gay before your wife did.

JAMES: Ah. Brenda. Course it's you.

BRENDA: Didn't recognise me without my pinny on?

JAMES: I just wasn't expecting to see you here. Thought you'd retired.

BRENDA: I have. Back's a mess. I can't bend down to pick up other people's shit any more.

JAMES: No, quite. Well, how lovely to see you.

PETER: Anybody enlighten us as to what "this" is all for then? Quite hard to dress appropriately when you don't know what it is you've been invited to.

JONATHAN: Julia thought maybe a birthday. How old is your father?

JAMES: Don't ask me. We never celebrated his birthdays. He was always away.

Don't you know, Julia?

JULIA: He would never say. Somewhere between 90 and 110, I'd say.

PETER: So it is a birthday party?

MARGARET enters.

MARGARET: Is this where we're supposed to be?

JAMES: Mummy! Do you know how old Dad is?

MARGARET thinks for a moment.

MARGARET: No.

JULIA: My mother would have known.

MARGARET: I'm sure she would.

JAMES greets his mother with a kiss.

JAMES: What are we all gathered for then?

MARGARET: You're asking me?

JULIA: You are married to him, Margaret.

MARGARET: Is that what you'd call it?

JONATHAN: So we're all in the dark? He must have mentioned something to you.

MARGARET: We've not been communicating very well recently. Not since his stroke.

A moment. None of the assembled knew anything about that.

JAMES: He had a stroke? You never said.

(To JULIA.) Did you know?

JULIA shakes her head.

MARGARET: You father doesn't want to seem as weak as the rest of us civilians.

Doesn't befit a former submarine commander.

PETER: Is he alright?

MARGARET: *(Scathing, to PETER.)* Oh, God, you're here are you?

PETER : *(To JAMES.)* That! You see, that's what I mean.

JAMES: How is he, Mum?

MARGARET: Put your shoes on will you, Brenda. Nobody wants to see your feet.

Am I wrong?

BRENDA: I've missed you too, Margaret.

PETER: I don't think I'm even invited.

JAMES: You're my partner. Of course you're invited.

PETER: My name wasn't on the invitation and our room was reserved for Mr. and Mrs. James Voss. I bet they've invited your bloody ex-wife.

219

JAMES: Don't be ridiculous. When did he have the stroke, Mum?

MARGARET: Oh don't keep asking me to remember dates.

JAMES: Weeks ago, months?

MARGARET: Yes, something like that.

JAMES: Which?

PETER: *(To JAMES.)* When did you last speak to him?

JAMES: I don't know. Not everybody phones home every Sunday night like they're still at boarding school. When did you last speak to him, Julia?

JULIA: I'd say it's been a good while.

JAMES: He didn't want you to tell us?

MARGARET: That's the feeling I got.

JAMES: Did he actually say that?

MARGARET: Difficult to say.

JULIA: Have you been nursing him back to health, Margaret?

MARGARET: I've been doing my best.

JULIA: Your best? Poor Daddy.

JONATHAN: So this is what? An after-stroke afterparty, party?

PETER: I definitely don't have an outfit for that.

JONATHAN: Or a "live life to the fullest while you can" party.

JULIA : Don't get any ideas.

BRENDA: Or an "I'm changing my will and giving all my money to the cleaner instead of you shitty bastards" party?

MARGARET: Oh God, no. He wouldn't, would he?

JULIA: He'd better not. Some of that money was my mother's. He's no right.

PAM enters.

PAM: Hello. Am I in the right place?

BRENDA: Oh, bloody hell!

MARGARET: Are any of us?

PAM: Hello, Ma'am.

MARGARET: Hello, Pam.

JULIA: Oh, her! Forgettable face to be fair - I'm not losing my mind yet.

PAM: *(To MARGARET.)* You look beautiful, Ma'am - lovely dress. Is it new?

MARGARET: Yes, it's rather splendid isn't it.

PAM: I bought a new frock too.

Expecting a compliment in return but not getting one...

MARGARET: Did you pack my vanity case? I can't find it in my room.

PAM: I haven't worked for you these past five years, Ma'am.

MARGARET: I keep forgetting. Our new girl looks so like you.

This jars for PAM but she recovers herself quickly.

PAM: I can have a look in your room if you'd like?

MARGARET: Would you?

BRENDA: I can't believe I'm hearing this.

PAM: It would be my pleasure.

PAM walks along and gives a little curtsy to PETER and JAMES.

When she gets to JULIA, she throws her arms around her.

JULIA: Oh. Goodness.

PAM: It's so good to see you, Ma'am. You look lovely.

JULIA: Yes, well. You can let go of me now.

PAM: Of course.

PAM curtsies to JONATHAN and then she gets to BRENDA, the only person sitting, feet outstretched on one of the chairs.

PAM (CONT'D): Brenda.

BRENDA: Aren't you going to give me a little curtsy and all?

PAM: What number room are you in, Ma'am? I'll hunt down your case. *(Pointedly at BRENDA.)* I'm only sorry nobody offered to help sooner.

MARGARET: Room 4, just down the corridor.

MARGARET holds out her key to PAM but BRENDA leans in and gets it.

PAM: I'm doing it. Not you.

MARGARET: As long as somebody does/

BRENDA: Neither of us is.

(To PAM.) We've not been invited here to work for free and if that's what they think, we're going to show them they're wrong.

PAM: I'm happy to do it. Give me the key.

BRENDA: No.

JONATHAN: I'll look for it. Give me the key.

BRENDA: Yes, let Jonathan go.

JULIA: Margaret doesn't need you rifling through her vanity case, Jonathan.

PAM: No need to bother yourself, Sir.

BRENDA: Bloody hell, Pam. Why shouldn't he go?

PETER: Well, I could go for that matter. If it would help.

JAMES: I don't think there's any need for you to/

BRENDA: Let one of them go.

PAM: Brenda, I'm asking nicely, will you please...

BRENDA waves the key in the air, taunting PAM who launches herself at BRENDA to get them. A scuffle ensues.

JONATHAN: Now hold on, I don't think there's any need for/

JAMES: Ladies, really/

MARGARET: This isn't helping my headache.

JULIA: Take an asprin.

MARGARET: I would but they are in my vanity case.

JULIA starts laughing. MARGARET joins in.

PAM: *(Mid-tussle.)* I will find it for you, Ma'am, if I can just/

ELIZABETH and GEORGE enter. They choose to ignore the scuffle and greet the family.

ELIZABETH : Margaret, how are you? How's my brother?

MARGARET : You'll have to ask him yourself, Elizabeth.

JAMES: Uncle George, you look well.

223

GEORGE: You too, young man. I've forgotten your name.

JAMES: James. I'm your nephew.

GEORGE: Of course, of course.

BRENDA: *(Mid-scuffle.)* You just scrammed me. There look, an actual red scram on my arm.

PAM: *(Mid-scuffle.)* Give me the key!

JAMES: This is Peter…

GEORGE: I don't think I've had the/

JAMES: My partner.

GEORGE: Oh. Did I know about that?

ELIZABETH: I reminded you ten minutes ago, George.

GEORGE: Ah yes. You did. You reminded me about James's "gay partner" and you told me not to mention Morven. Because they're not married anymore. You see, I remember more than you think.

BRENDA is running around the table away from PAM who is chasing her. PAM does a little curtsy for the benefit of ELIZABETH and GEORGE.

PAM: *(To ELIZABETH.)* Lovely dress, Ma'am.

BRENDA: I'm faster than you, I am. I always was.

PAM: You've never been faster than me. You used to work like a snail. Only time I ever saw you move fast was when it was going home time.

BRENDA: I was quicker than you at cleaning silver.

PAM: You were slap-dash.

ELIZABETH: Pleased to meet you, Peter.

PETER: Hello.

ELIZABETH: You can call me Aunty if you like.

PETER: Oh, thank you.

ELIZABETH: *(Still to PETER.)* Look at your shirt. Look George, isn't his shirt… interesting?

GEORGE: It reminds me of the curtains my mother hung in our downstairs lavatory.

Happy memories.

ELIZABETH: How are you, Julia? You look cross as always.

JULIA: I probably am.

ELIZABETH: What are you cross about now?

JULIA: The list is endless.

GEORGE: Not too cross to say hello to your Uncle George.

JULIA: Of course not.

GEORGE and JULIA kiss in greeting.

PETER: *(To ELIZABETH.)* I think I've met your son, Elizabeth.

ELIZABETH's demeanor changes rapidly. Suddenly very grave. PETER thinks it's because he called her Elizabeth.

PETER (CONT'D): Sorry I mean, Aunty. I forgot.

ELIZABETH: My son?

PETER: In Venice.

JAMES: You're getting confused. That was Andrew.

PETER: Your cousin.

JAMES: No, he's the son of Mum's best friend.

MARGARET: How is Andrew?

PETER: I'm always getting things wrong. Sorry. So do you not have any children?

ELIZABETH doesn't answer.

GEORGE: What's that? Children? Us? No. Unless you count the dogs. Two beautiful Cocker Spaniels. Wanted to bring them with us but travelling doesn't agree with little SheShe.

ELIZABETH: SheShe died three years ago, George.

JONATHAN: Oh, what a shame!

GEORGE: No?! Could have sworn I gave her a Trixie Roller Pop just this morning.

BRENDA: Come on then if you want it.

PAM: Give me that!

MARGARET: Will somebody please do something about those women?

ANUSHKA enters with a tureen of soup.

ELIZABETH: Where is Edward?

JAMES: Did you know about the stroke, Aunty?

ELIZABETH: What? Yes. Of course I did.

GEORGE: I haven't had a stroke, damn it. Is that what you think, James?

ELIZABETH: Edward, George.

GEORGE: That's not Edward, Elizabeth. That's Edward's son. Christ. And you tell me my memory is going.

ELIZABETH: Edward's stroke.

GEORGE: Oh yes, I forgot about that.

BRENDA: You're fitter than you look, you are Pam. Fair play. I'm cream crackered.

JAMES: How is he?

PAM: Agghhhhh.

PAM charges at her and nearly collides with ANUSHKA and the tureen of soup but ANUSHKA makes an elegant side-step. JONATHAN gives her a round of applause.

JONATHAN: Bravo! Well saved.

ANUSHKA gives JONATHAN a dismissive look.

BRENDA: Cor, Pam. You're like a raging bull.

PAM charges at her again. OSCAR, enters laden with wild flowers he has picked on his walk. BRENDA runs around him, PAM in pursuit.

OSCAR: Whoa, time, ladies, what's the hurry? Your Alan Whickers on fire or something?

BRENDA: *(While running.)* Alright Oscar. You still singing to the flowers?

OSCAR: Course I am. Cheers them up.

BRENDA: *(Still running.)* Stretch your leg out and trip this one up will you, then I can say hello properly.

OSCAR: I wouldn't want to make Pam fall. Unless it was in love with me.

PAM stops.

BRENDA: He's only playing with you, Pam. Everybody knows Oscar Kelly'll never be married to anything but his garden.

PAM: Hello Oscar.

PAM gives OSCAR a kiss of greeting.

BRENDA: Made her stop though. Fair play. Better than tripping her up.

PAM launches herself at BRENDA, who flees the room. PAM follows.

JAMES: Was Dad in a bad way when you saw him, Aunty?

GEORGE: Your father doesn't worry about disease or illness. He's a Navy man – he'll go down with his ship.

JAMES: He hasn't commanded a submarine for over twenty years, Uncle.

GEORGE: I know that. *(To ELIZABETH.)* Does he think I'm losing my marbles? *(To JAMES.)* Your father will be the last of us standing. He'll hold on until global warming submerges the whole damn planet.

OSCAR: Hello ladies and gents.

OSCAR goes round the group handing out wild flowers to the ladies. To ELIZABETH.

OSCAR (CONT'D): Ladies' Bedstraw for you Ma'am, to match your smile.

ELIZABETH: Thank you, Oscar. How kind.

OSCAR: Cornflower for you Ma'am. Sets off your eyes.

MARGARET: Yes, I do suit blue.

OSCAR gives MARGARET the flower, leaving just JULIA.

OSCAR: And for you/

JULIA: What? A white rose to match my complexion, or a red one to tone with my lips?

OSCAR: A thistle.

JULIA: Charming.

OSCAR: Prickly but beautiful.

OSCAR holds the flower out. JULIA doesn't take it so JONATHAN does.

JONATHAN: It is beautiful. *(To JULIA.)* You could wear it in your hair. Like this.

JONATHAN puts it behind his ear.

OSCAR: Quite fetching, Sir.

JULIA: I don't think it's a flowers-in-your-hair kind of occasion, Jonathan.

JULIA takes it out of JONATHAN's hair.

JONATHAN: More's the pity.

ELIZABETH: What did Brenda mean about you singing to the flowers, Oscar?

OSCAR: It's my secret weapon, Ma'am. Helps them grow good and strong. I brought a Bougainvillea back from the brink by singing it "Build Me Up Buttercup".

ELIZABETH: I sing to George, sometimes. To get him back on track. It's very lonely when the one person who shares all your memories starts to lose them.

GEORGE: What's that?

ELIZABETH: Nothing.

JULIA turns her attention to ANUSHKA who has begun serving soup for each table setting.

JULIA: Why's she serving soup now? We're not all gathered.

OSCAR: Didn't need to sing out there. Everything's thriving. Still sang a tune or two though. Because it was all so beautiful.

OSCAR finds a vase and begins arranging the rest of his pickings.

JULIA: Tell her Jonathan.

JONATHAN: What should I say?

JULIA: Tell her she's early.

JONATHAN: I don't want to be rude.

PETER: I'll tell her. Important to get the timings right at this sort of occasion.

JAMES: Says the man who's ALWAYS late.

PETER: Early people never credit the fact that sometimes being late is preferable to being early.

JULIA: Tell her, if you're going to tell her.

PETER sidles up to ANUSHKA.

JAMES: Where is Dad?

PETER: I'm sorry but, you're a little early with the soup.

ANUSHKA continues to serve up.

ELIZABETH: We've not seen him yet.

GEORGE: Dropped off our bags and came straight here.

PETER: Excuse me. Hello. Sorry, I think you might want to stop serving the soup.

Is she hard of hearing or something? TOO SOON! NO SOUP YET.

ANUSHKA looks up, gives him a blank look and continues to serve up. PETER gives up.

JAMES: Where is Dad, Mum?

MARGARET: I don't know.

JAMES: When did you both arrive?

MARGARET: The doctor didn't think he should fly so...

JAMES: So you came by train?

MARGARET: Of course not. You know how travel sick trains make me. I flew.

Your father came by train.

JAMES: Mum!

JULIA: All heart, aren't you Margaret?

MARGARET: He's fine. He has his nurse with him.

JULIA: Not very effective are you.

(To JAMES.) Your wife would have had everything organised before she'd said hello.

JAMES: Don't let's talk about Morven.

PETER: *(Aside to JAMES.)* You said your sister hated your ex-wife.

JAMES: She does.

JULIA: I do not and have not ever hated Morven, have I Jonathan?

JONATHAN: Um, well/

JAMES: You used to call her Ninnyhammer.

JULIA: That was Daddy's name for her.

JAMES: You used to say you'd rather force your fist down a blender than spend an evening with her.

JULIA: I feel that about most people.

JONATHAN: She does.

231

JAMES: You once asked me, totally sincerely, if she had blackmailed me into marrying her.

JULIA: I thought you could do better. That was before you brought home/

JAMES: *(Warning her.)* Julia…

PETER: Me? You were going to say me?

JONATHAN: Oh deary me.

Turning her attention to ANUSHKA.

JULIA: Excuse me. That won't do. You'll have to take it all away and heat it up.

ANUSHKA serves up the last bowl and walks past JULIA.

JULIA (CONT'D): Excuse me!

ANUSHKA stops and turns and, with a strong Eastern European accent, declares.

ANUSHKA: GAZ. PACH. O.

She exits.

ELIZABETH: Oh I love gazpacho.

JULIA: What a rude woman.

ELIZABETH: Remember that time in Gibraltar, George? The waiter's face when you sent it back.

GEORGE: Have I been to Gibraltar?

JULIA: She could have said earlier.

ELIZABETH: Several times.

I'm going to start.

ELIZABETH makes her way to the table.

232

JULIA: Just rude.

ELIZABETH: Does she mean me? I have to eat regularly or
my blood sugar gets too low.

GEORGE: It's true.

JULIA: Don't you think?

JONATHAN: Yes darling, it was. Quite rude really.

ELIZABETH: You're the same. *(To the others about GEORGE.)*
He gets terribly grumpy.

PETER: Did you not tell them about my allergies when you
told them I'm vegetarian?

JAMES: You'll be fine.

GEORGE: Maybe I'll join you then. If nobody minds.

MARGARET: Where are those women with my key?

PETER: You know my body cannot tolerate tomatoes.

JAMES: So you say.

GEORGE joins ELIZABETH at the table and tucks into the soup.

PETER: I've had tests! Did you tell them?

JAMES : You expect people to bend over backwards to
accommodate you and then I catch you scoffing your
"danger foods" in secret and you say, "It won't hurt this
once."

PETER: You promised me you'd tell them.

JAMES: I lied.

ELIZABETH: It's good, isn't it? Tastes like summer.

One by one, during the ensuing quarrel between PETER and JAMES, the assembled guests – JONATHAN, JULIA, MARGARET and OSCAR take a seat and begin eating their soup.

PETER: Gazpacho. I mean that's literally the worst thing they could serve me.

JAMES: So eat some bread.

PETER: It's got olives in it!

ELIZABETH: Oh has it? Delicious. Pass me some would you, Jonathan.

JONATHAN : It's very good. Try it, Julia.

JAMES: I don't think you're going to starve.

PETER: I am in the correct weight range for my body actually.

JAMES: I wasn't…

JONATHAN: *(To JULIA about the bread.)* Well?

JULIA: Not bad.

PETER: Whenever we're with your family, you become super-critical of me. Just because your family struggle to accept me doesn't mean/

JAMES: Please don't make this about you.

ELIZABETH: Doesn't she like it?

JONATHAN: "Not bad" is high praise from Julia. She loves it, don't you darling?

PETER: Oh sorry, was I detracting attention from you for two minutes?!

JAMES : I've just found out my father's had a stroke!

MARGARET: Yes, quite tasty really. The garlic really pings out.

234

JAMES: What's that look for?

PETER: You can't pull that card with me.

JAMES: What's that supposed to mean?

PETER: Forget it.

GEORGE: It'd be better warm though, wouldn't it? I mean, this is Scotland not Seville.

JAMES: No. Tell me.

PETER: You're like strangers. You told me that. How upsetting is it to find out a stranger's had a stroke?

JAMES is wounded.

PETER (CONT'D): I'm sorry, that didn't/

JAMES: Sometimes I hate you, you know.

OSCAR: I thought it was actually surprisingly balmy. My first time across the border. Didn't know what to expect. Bought a pair of long johns specially.

Not sure about this soup though.

PETER walks away.

JAMES: Where are you going?

PETER: I'm going to change my shirt.

PETER exits leaving JAMES standing awkwardly.

MARGARET: Aren't you going to join us?

JAMES: Shouldn't we be waiting for Dad?

GEORGE: He's late.

JAMES: No.

GEORGE: My watch says thirty-two minutes past.

JAMES: Two minutes isn't/

GEORGE: In the Navy it is.

JULIA: He isn't in the Navy anymore, Uncle George, and his wife has left him travelling the breadth of the country on his own.

MARGARET: He has a nurse.

JULIA: Oh well, that's alright then isn't it?

ELIZABETH: What do you think of her, Margaret? The nurse?

GEORGE: That's a leading question if ever I/

ELIZABETH: I'm just asking Margaret what/

GEORGE: Because you took a dislike to/

ELIZABETH: I merely thought she/

GEORGE: She was just doing her job. She's supposed to be/

ELIZABETH: I don't think she is. You forget I was a nurse in the/

GEORGE: I haven't forgotten.

ELIZABETH: And I… well, I look after you.

GEORGE: We look after each other, don't we?

A moment.

ELIZABETH: Yes of course.

I'd just like to know what Margaret thinks of her?

MARGARET: I haven't really spoken to her.

ELIZABETH: How's that possible?

MARGARET: I don't know Elizabeth, I find the whole thing very…

GEORGE: Not spoken to her?

MARGARET: Very…

ELIZABETH: She's been looking after him for/

MARGARET: Very…

GEORGE: That is surprising/

MARGARET: Embarrassing.

A little muffled cough. EDWARD is in the room, sitting in a wheelchair, pushed by THE NURSE. EDWARD is clutching a parcel, which remains on his chair throughout.

GIOVANNI stands behind. They are surprised to see everybody already eating. A number of the group are surprised to see EDWARD so diminished. It's pretty awkward all round.

JAMES: You're here!

MARGARET: I didn't tell people to start.

JONATHAN: We were all a little peckish, I'm afraid.

ELIZABETH: You know what I'm like.

MARGARET: They all just sat down. It was rather a case of it being rude NOT to join them.

EDWARD doesn't move or say anything.

MARGARET (CONT'D): Don't just hover there. Come on.

ELIZABETH: The soup is very good.

EDWARD leans back and whispers to THE NURSE.

EDWARD: *(Inaudible.)* Let's eat then.

THE NURSE listens and nods. Silence from the rest of the room.

She is about to wheel him forward when PAM pushes past holding MARGARET's vanity case. BRENDA is pulling on it, trying to prevent PAM from taking it in to the room.

PAM: Give. It. Here.

PAM gives an almighty tug, pulling the case out of BRENDA's grasp. Both women stumble. BRENDA recovers herself and sees EDWARD for the first time.

BRENDA: Bloody hell, the last five years haven't been kind to you, have they?

PAM recovers herself and gives a little curtsy to EDWARD.

PAM: Sir.

PAM then presents the vanity case to MARGARET like it is a great treasure.

MARGARET: What's this for?

PAM: I found it for you, Ma'am.

MARGARET: Well I don't need it at the dinner table, do I?

PAM is deflated. This is all watched by BRENDA.

PAM: No Ma'am. I'll put it back in your room.

BRENDA: *(Gentler than before.)* You'll put it on the side and sit down at the table with the other GUESTS.

The fight has gone out of PAM. She does as BRENDA says, placing the case on the side and laying the key on top of it. She sits down to eat her soup. BRENDA sits down too, turning her attention to EDWARD as she tucks into her starter.

BRENDA (CONT'D): You not going to sit down then? You're already sitting down right enough but are you going to join us at the dinner table or stay over there watching us?

A moment. EDWARD smiles. Then gives a little nod. THE NURSE wheels him to the table.

GIOVANNI follows.

GIOVANNI: Hello everybody. Edward is my dear friend. We have connected with our souls. It is a privilege to be here amongst you all.

THE NURSE has set EDWARD at the table and helped him to anything he might need. He gestures to THE NURSE and GIOVANNI to sit, which they do.

Everybody eats soup, EDWARD with more difficulty than the others, holding his serviette close to wipe round his face where he spills.

PETER enters wearing a different (more hideous) shirt and realises everybody has arrived.

PETER: Sorry everybody.

He goes to sit down. There's no seat for him.

PETER (CONT'D): Oh. There's no seat for me.

(Aside to JAMES.) I told you I wasn't invited.

GIOVANNI: It is my fault. I was not expected here tonight.

PAM: I'll sort you out.

BRENDA: Course you will.

PAM sorts PETER out a place at the table. While PETER waits…

PETER: *(Aside to JAMES about his shirt.)* This is better, isn't it? It feels better.

JAMES doesn't answer.

239

Oh God, is it not better?

JAMES: It's fine.

JAMES sees the anxiety on PETER's face.

You look very handsome.

PETER: Good. Ok. Thank you.

PAM has set PETER a place.

Thank you, Pam.

PETER sniffs at the soup, rejects it.

Have I missed the toast?

JAMES: Stop complaining about the food.

PETER : I mean the raise a glass toast not/

GEORGE: Good point, young man. Is there to be no toast?

JULIA: Yes, Daddy. When are you going to tell us why you've gathered us all here?

JONATHAN: Is it a birthday celebration?

ELIZABETH: Edward's birthday's not until November. It's a wedding anniversary, isn't it?

MARGARET: Whose?

ELIZABETH: Yours of course.

MARGARET: Ours is September. Unless it's his and Sophie's.

GEORGE: Sophie's dead isn't she?

ELIZABETH: Yes, George. She died a long time ago.

GEORGE: That's what I thought. Never heard of anybody celebrating their anniversary to their dead first wife. That would be a little/

JULIA: It's not their anniversary. They were married in February.

JAMES: Well, Dad? Why are we all here?

BRENDA: Maybe he just missed seeing all our ugly mugs?

OSCAR: Or wanted to give us the gift of this beautiful scenery, is that right Mr. Voss? I'll keep these hills with me when I'm trimming the hedges back home, I'll tell you that for nothing.

GIOVANNI: My friend, Edward, is a very generous man.

PETER: It is beautiful out there. Though some of the steps are a bit treacherous, nearly broke my back when we arrived.

JULIA: A thing can't be treacherous. Only a person.

MARGARET: Is that it Edward? You've brought us all here for a holiday? Do tell us.

JONATHAN: Speech!

PETER: I really can't say anything, can I?

JAMES: Oh do shut up, Peter.

GEORGE: Speech!

ELIZABETH: *(Reminding GEORGE that EDWARD can't make a speech.)* George!

GEORGE: What? Oh yes, I forgot.

OSCAR: Yeah, got to have a Holy Ghost at dinner!

JONATHAN: Holy Ghost?

OSCAR: Toast!

BRENDA: Go on, mun, give us a speech!

Clinking of glasses and "Speech, speech" from most of the assembled (except ELIZABETH, GEORGE, MARGARET and THE NURSE who know the extent of EDWARD's communication difficulties.)

An expectant silence. EDWARD uses all his energy to push himself up to standing. He surveys the room, takes a deep breath and...

EDWARD's speech is unintelligible. His voice is small and weak, his words are slurred beyond recognition. He seems oblivious to the shock on the faces of his assembled family.

EDWARD : *(Unintelligible.)* Thank you. Travelling. Bonny Scotland. Beautiful. Cold Scotland. Scots don't mind cold. Stand outside. With glasses. Nip in air.

He pauses for a moment and THE NURSE laughs out loud. She is surprised that the rest of the room do not. Seeing their confusion, she explains what EDWARD said as if it was perfectly clear and they are fools not to have understood.

THE NURSE: It was a joke. He said the Scots'll stand outside with their glass held aloft if you tell them there's a nip in the air.

JONATHAN: Oh yes, very good.

PAM: That's a good one, Sir.

JAMES: Good one, Dad.

EDWARD realises nobody can understand a word. He sits, dejected.

GEORGE starts clapping.

GEORGE: Well done, Edward.

JONATHAN : Absolutely.

GEORGE: Good health.

JONATHAN: Bon appetit!

OSCAR: All the hairy chest to you, Mr. Voss.

BRENDA: Iechyd Da!

JAMES stands and raises his glass.

JAMES: Cheers Dad.

Others join in making a toast.

JULIA: Cheers.

PAM: Your good health, Mr Voss.

GIOVANNI: Cincin.

All are standing now, their glasses raised towards EDWARD. EDWARD stands and reaches for his glass. Instead of raising it, he downs it in one. Everybody sits. Almost immediately EDWARD stands again. This confuses PAM. She stands, realises nobody else is standing but EDWARD and sits again.

All eyes on a very thoughtful EDWARD. He gestures to THE NURSE. She leans in to him.

He speaks an inaudible whisper into her ear, she translates.

EDWARD: *(Unintelligible.)* Why raise glasses? No toast. No speaker. Even strong voice and mouth. Form the words.

THE NURSE: Why did you raise your glasses? I hadn't made a toast. I've never been a speaker. Even when my voice was strong and my mouth could form the words.

GEORGE: That's not true, Edward. You did a cracking best man speech at our wedding.

ELIZABETH: That was Mark not Edward. Mark was your best man.

GEORGE: Was he? Oh, yes, you could be right. Sorry everybody. Do continue.

EDWARD starts again. THE NURSE translates.

EDWARD: *(Unintelligible, whispered into THE NURSE's ear.)* My life. Blurred. Long goodbye. Meal.

THE NURSE : My life has blurred into one long goodbye meal.

JULIA: Last Repasts you used to call them.

JAMES: The last suppers we'd have together before you were deployed.

JULIA: I hated them.

JONATHAN holds JULIA's hand.

MARGARET: So did I.

GEORGE: Are you being deployed again, Edward?

ELIZABETH: The year is 2017, George. Edward hasn't been in active service for a long time. Do try to remember.

EDWARD raises his glass.

EDWARD: *(Unintelligible.)* To. Final command!

THE NURSE : To my final command!

GIOVANNI: To your final command, Signor Edward!

GEORGE: Here, here – to your final command!

(To ELIZABETH.) You see, he is being deployed again.

Some of the others join in uncertainly, PAM and OSCAR, PETER... "To your final command".

JAMES: What does he mean? His final command. Mum?

MARGARET: I'm not exactly sure.

ELIZABETH: That is a rather odd toast, Edward. What does it mean?

GIOVANNI: Signor Edward is choosing to die tonight.

MARGARET: What?

GIOVANNI: I am in love with his courage.

JULIA: Excuse me, what are you talking about?

GIOVANNI: Today. Your father, yes? He chooses to die.

MARGARET: Don't be ridiculous.

ELIZABETH: You can't just choose to die.

JAMES: I don't understand what's going on.

MARGARET: Why would he want to do that?

GIOVANNI: He has terrible pain.

ELIZABETH: Nonsense. I spoke to his doctor. Edward's reported pain levels were very low. Us Vosses have a high pain threshold. We always have.

GEORGE: What's going on, Elizabeth?

GIOVANNI: Signor Edward's pain is in his heart.

ELIZABETH: Who is this man? Will somebody please tell him to shut up?

JULIA: Are you going to enlighten us, Daddy or is this some sort of naval sport? Get your crew ready for a missile launch so you can laugh at them while they run around like headless chickens.

GIOVANNI: Your father is a clever man. He has used his money and his clever brain to find a website that will provide the help he needs.

PETER: Dignitas.

JAMES: Oh God. You've not?

ELIZABETH: He better not have.

GIOVANNI: What is this Dignitas?

MARGARET: This is nonsense, surely?

JULIA: This is awful.

OSCAR: *(Answering GIOVANNI.)* It's er, you know. Where you er go if you, you know.

PAM: It's a place you can go to die.

BRENDA: Bloody hell, mun. I didn't know what to expect from tonight but this wasn't it.

GIOVIANNI: No. No Dignitas. Not for Signor Edward. He has… what is the word?

ELIZABETH: Too much sense?

GIOVANNI: No, he has…

JAMES: His family.

JULIA: A cruel sense of humour.

GIOVANNI: Barbiturates.

JONATHAN: Bloody hell.

GIOVANNI: He will take them here tonight after dinner. With our love all around him. And we will all say goodbye. It is a very beautiful thing.

JAMES: Is that true?

MARGARET: Of course it isn't.

JULIA: Daddy?

EDWARD places the package he has been clutching on the table and pulls out a small bottle of liquid medicine (Nembutal) and an anti-nausea pill. Everybody stares at it.

Silence.

Interrupted by MORVEN, who runs in late. Everybody is too shell-shocked to say anything.

MORVEN: Oh God, you've all sat down. You're very prompt. I was hoping it was a 7.30 for 8 sort of thing. I'm so sorry. I got lost. I knew I should have taken the A9 but I ended up on all the little roads and then I got stuck behind a learner driver for about three miles. Of course I did. I'm the woman who always picks the slowest checkout at the supermarket. Delays seem to surround me like moths to a flame. Hello Edward. Thank you so much for inviting me.

She kisses EDWARD on the cheek but doesn't wait for a return greeting.

MORVEN (CONT'D): I'm glad you've all started because I'm starving and I never go for that standing around with a drink and nibbles thing because the wine just goes to my head that way. I like a glass of wine with my meal best of all. Hello James.

She kisses JAMES on the cheek.

MORVEN (CONT'D): What are you eating? Soup. Oh dear, cold now probably.

She dips her finger in JAMES's soup and taste it.

Gazpacho! A stroke of luck for once. Lovely.

(With an edge.) Hello Peter. That's quite a shirt.

247

I won't kiss everybody if you don't mind. I'm going to tuck in. Kisses to you all of course.

MORVEN blows kisses around the room.

Oh dear, no table setting. Had you given up on me so soon? Not to worry. I'll squeeze in between James and Peter. Pam, is that a spare bowl? And could you pass the bread? You're a dear. Ooo, olives. Delicious.

MORVEN has now sat down. A few mouthfuls in, she realises nobody has said anything.

MORVEN (CONT'D): Is everything alright? What's wrong? There's an atmosphere. I'm very sensitive about these things. James?

JAMES: It's Dad. He's…

MORVEN: Edward?

EDWARD leans in to THE NURSE and whispers.

THE NURSE translates.

THE NURSE: Hello, Ninnyhammer. Glad you could come.

Blackout.

THE NURSE

Out of time and place.

THE NURSE: I nursed my mother before I learnt to read.

I nursed my daughter. At my breast and later, when her blood was poisoning her. I nursed her then too.

Now I nurse strangers. Men and women in pain.

I wash their skin. I feed them. I soothe them.

I am their legs. I am their touch. And sometimes, I am their voice.

AFTER THE MISSILE

We're back in the room. Only a few moments have passed.

MORVEN has been let in on EDWARD's plan.

MORVEN: I didn't know.

JAMES: None of us knew.

MORVEN: Barbiturates? Bloody hell.

PAM is stacking plates.

BRENDA: Leave it, mun.

PAM: It calms me down.

OSCAR: Pass me some plates then. If it works for her…

A shaken OSCAR starts stacking plates too.

BRENDA: Ach-y-fi!

(To PAM.) Not one of them will thank you for it. You're invisible to them.

PAM: That's not true.

BRENDA raises an eyebrow.

JONATHAN: *(To JULIA.)* Are you alright?

BRENDA: Pass me the wine, will you?

JONATHAN: You look a bit flushed. Why don't you take off your cardigan?

PAM pours JULIA a glass of water and holds it out for her.

PAM: Perhaps a drink of water would/

JULIA: *(To JONATHAN.)* Why, so you can wear it? Would you like my earrings as well?

JONATHAN takes the water and downs it himself, without a thank you to PAM.

PETER: Why is it on the table?

JAMES: This is…

PETER: The medicine. Is he planning to do it here? In front of us.

JAMES: I can't believe this is happening.

JAMES is upset. Instead of comforting him, PETER walks past him towards EDWARD.

PAM is concerned for JAMES and pours him a glass a water, which she holds it out for him.

PETER: Excuse me, Edward. Where are you going to do it? Because if the plan is to do it here, in front of us all, well, we could be culpable. Legally speaking.

JAMES: *(To PAM about the water glass.)* Would you please stop thrusting that in my face.

A wounded PAM busies herself with clearing up.

PETER: I mean it's assisted suicide, isn't it?

EDWARD tries to respond.

EDWARD: *(Unintelligible.)* I will… My intention is to… I do not want to…

PETER cannot understand him.

PETER: Pardon. Sorry I didn't… Nope. I didn't get any of that.

JULIA: What's he doing? What are you doing?

PETER: We could get into trouble. We could be prosecuted. All of us.

MORVEN: Now, Peter…

JULIA: *(To JAMES.)* Will you tell your "partner" to leave our father alone.

JONATHAN: He's got a point though.

PETER: I don't want to go to jail.

MORVEN: I'm experienced in crisis management and you're not helping, Peter.

JULIA: None of us is going to jail.

JAMES: How exactly are you experienced in crisis management?

MORVEN: I did a Open University course in it.

A snort of derision from JAMES at this.

PETER: If he does it here, in front of us all/

JULIA: What are they going to do – arrest all of us?

PAM: Oh dear, could they?

BRENDA: They better bloody not.

PETER: I'm just saying that if we stand by and do nothing we could be seen as/

MORVEN: You need to breathe. This is bordering on a panic attack.

JONATHAN: I suppose there is safety in numbers.

PETER: I'm not so sure.

MORVEN: Does anybody have a paper bag?

251

JONATHAN: In a way, we're witnesses that nobody helped him so long as he takes it all unassisted. Presumably he procured the barbituates himself?

JULIA: I don't bloody know, Jonathan.

PETER: It's… we're… I'm not sure I want to be here.

MORVEN: Here, breathe into my napkin.

MORVEN thrusts her napkin at PETER, who wasn't having a panic attack before but is struggling to breathe now thanks to MORVEN.

JONATHAN: Did you order the barbiturates yourself, Edward? Actually, don't answer that. The less we all know, the better, probably.

PETER finally manages to push away MORVEN and her napkin.

PETER: I am not having a panic attack!

JONATHAN: So long as nobody assists in any way/

ELIZABETH: Please could everybody stop talking like this is happening. It's not happening.

PETER: I just don't like this. Not one bit.

JULIA: None of us does, you retard.

MORVEN: Now, Julia…

PETER: Why is everybody so awful to me?

MORVEN: That sort of negative energy isn't going to help anything.

JULIA: Why are you even here?

MORVEN: I was invited.

JULIA: Why?

JAMES: Yes, why?

DOWN THE HATCH

MORVEN: I'm family.

JULIA: Not anymore.

JAMES: Not for a decade…

MORVEN: Edward's very fond of me.

PAM is clearing up near MORVEN, whispers a quiet compliment.

PAM: Lovely outfit, Ma'am.

MORVEN: It was a wonderful bargain. All my girlfriends
    wanted it but I'm the only one who can fit into a size 10.

PETER: He invited her instead of me.

JAMES: Now's not the/

PETER: They weren't expecting me. Count the place settings.

JAMES: Of course they were expecting you.

PETER: Your father still doesn't accept me.

ELIZABETH: This is not happening. It's not. Do you hear me,
    Edward? THIS IS NOT HAPPENING!

This outburst leaves ELIZABETH feeling dizzy. GEORGE catches her.

GEORGE: Elizabeth, you need to breathe. Deep breaths.

MORVEN: Does she want to breathe into my napkin.

JAMES/JULIA: NO!

MORVEN: Goodness me.

(To PETER.) He was never this tetchy when we were
    together.

PETER: What's that supposed to mean?

MORVEN shrugs her shoulders.

GEORGE: Why don't we step out? Get some air.

ELIZABETH: You don't get to choose. You told me that. No matter how much pain we're in. You don't get to choose.

GEORGE: When did I tell you that?

ELIZABETH: I held him in my arms and you said/

GEORGE: Who? Who did you hold?

ELIZABETH: How can you...?

ELIZABETH is devastated that GEORGE does not remember.

MARGARET: This is all...

I'm going to get to the bottom of this. Everybody calm down.

MARGARET makes her way towards EDWARD. When she gets there, she's suddenly not sure what to say.

MARGARET (CONT'D): What's this all about, Edward?

EDWARD leans in to THE NURSE and starts speaking for her to translate.

MARGARET (CONT'D): Not her. Speak to me. I don't need a translator.

EDWARD leans in and speaks a few unintelligible words into MARGARET's ear.

EDWARD: *(Unintelligible.)* Can't live. This. Sorry.

MARGARET, having set herself up and aware of being watched, doesn't want to let on that she hasn't a clue what he's just said.

MARGARET: Yes, well quite.

Just pass that by me again a little louder this time.

EDWARD leans in again and whispers.

254

EDWARD: *(Unintelligible.)* Is… is… impossible.

MARGARET is none the wiser.

She feels the weight of everybody's eyes on her.

MARGARET: He says… he's says… he says there's been a misunderstanding.

EDWARD makes some noises of complaint.

EDWARD: *(Unintelligible.)* No. Not say/

MARGARET: He says that the last thing he would ever want to do, EVER, is to upset his family.

EDWARD is chastened. Listens to MARGARET who's getting into her stride now.

MARGARET (CONT'D): He says he loves us all too much. He says he loves me very much.

Something shifts in MARGARET. Having lived for so many years desperate for EDWARD to communicate with her, she finds this projection of what he might say to her seductive and therapeutic. It escalates without her even being fully conscious that she's saying this aloud to the room.

He says he loves me desperately. Hopelessly. Deeply.

He says he's sorry we haven't had the marriage we should have. He doesn't blame me for it going wrong.

He says he shouldn't have courted me at my father's funeral. That when a sixteen year old slip of a thing makes a play for a sad-eyed widower looking dashing in his uniform, the responsibility lies with the adult to say "no". He should never have asked me to marry him when I had seen so little of the world. He shouldn't have made me tie myself to him and mother his daughter when I was so young.

An indignant snort from JULIA.

MARGARET (CONT'D): He says I have given too much in our marriage and he has given too little.

He says he wishes he'd told me all this before his stroke. He wishes he'd set me free. He says/

OSCAR: Blimey, he said all of that really quickly, didn't he? Only took him a few seconds.

JULIA: Stop it Margaret.

MORVEN: He didn't say any of that, did he?

MARGARET snaps out of her reverie.

MARGARET: He did with his eyes.

MORVEN: Knew it. I've a sense for these things.

ANUSKHA enters and gathers together the stacked plates. From the moment EDWARD sees her, he is spellbound.

MARGARET: Am I right, Edward? Tell me I'm right.

ANUSHKA exits with plates. EDWARD rises to his feet and holds out his arms towards her. He is not strong enough to follow. He says something. He says it again. Over and over. It is unintelligible.

EDWARD: *(Unintelligible.)* Sophie.

ELIZABETH: What's he saying?

MARGARET: Say it louder, Edward. Clearer. Try. Please.

EDWARD: *(Unintelligible.)* Sophie. Sophie.

OSCAR: What's he saying?

BRENDA: Don't ask me, Mun.

EDWARD: *(Unintelligible.)* Sophie.

MARGARET: What? I don't understand. Tell me.

What's he saying? What's he saying!

THE NURSE is attending to EDWARD, trying to soothe him. MARGARET throws a bread roll at the back of her head.

THE NURSE : Oh, my.

MARGARET: Tell me what he's saying?

EDWARD: *(Unintelligible.)* Sophie.

THE NURSE: Can't you tell? It's clear as day.

MARGARET: I don't understand him. I never have. Not now, not ever.

THE NURSE : He's saying, Sophie.

This winds MARGARET.

ANUSHKA reenters with the main course and begins serving it, oblivious of EDWARD's gaze.

EDWARD: *(Unintelligible.)* Sophie. Sophie. You?

The others turn to look at ANUSHKA.

PAM: She does have a look of her.

OSCAR: How she'd have looked if she'd lived, bless her soul.

JULIA: I can't see it at all.

ANUSHKA realises everybody is staring at her.

ANUSHKA: Chick. En.

She starts to leave. EDWARD becomes agitated and begins banging things. He grabs a candlestick and a fork and clangs it repeatedly until ANUSHKA turns, surprised at the banging. He keeps banging until it slowly dawns on her that it's for her benefit. She walks up to him.

EDWARD: *(Unintelligible.)* Sophie. Me. Edward.

ANUSHKA: NO SPEAK ENGLISH.

ANUSHKA gives an apologetic shrug of the shoulders and exits.

MARGARET: Is this about her? Your wife killed herself over fifty years ago. I think it's a little late to try to follow her now, don't you?

EDWARD: *(Unintelligible.)* So. Like her.

MARGARET: I don't understand you!

Upset, MARGARET gets out her mobile phone and makes a call.

JULIA makes her way to EDWARD.

JULIA: Is this about Mummy?

EDWARD holds his hand out to JULIA, full of affection.

MARGARET: *(Into her phone.)* I need you...

I know we said later but...

I. Need. You.

JULIA: She left me playing on the sand. She blew a kiss at me and then waded out into the ocean. She wanted to find you. Join you in your submarine. She longed for you so. Did she come knocking for you? Did you hear her floating past the boat deep, deep down in the black?

You came home and I thought I had you then. Swapped her for you. A child can only lose one parent to the sea, can't she? And then you went back.

Back to your underwater coffin where nobody could reach you. And left me all alone.

You never spoke to me about her. Not once. Talk to me now. Talk to me about my mother.

Everybody waits on EDWARD. EDWARD says nothing.

JULIA (CONT'D): *(To THE NURSE.)* What's he saying?

THE NURSE: Nothing.

JULIA: Then what's he thinking?

THE NURSE : I don't know.

JULIA looks at her father expectantly. Nothing.

JULIA: Fuck you!

JULIA runs off.

JONATHAN: Julia!

JONATHAN goes to follow JULIA. He stops in front of EDWARD, gives an accusatory look, a tut, a shake of the head, then exits after JULIA.

BRENDA: I read about this woman in America who had a death party. She was an artist. Invited all her friends like it was a wedding then topped herself at the top of a hill. I remember thinking at the time, what the hell do you wear to a do like that?

MORVEN: There's so much sadness in this room. I'm very sensitive to sadness.

BRENDA: She told the people she invited what they were coming to, mind you. Set the ground rules. No crying in front of her, no aggro at all. So her last hours were really nice, you know, people saying nice things and laughing.

Might have been better if you'd have warned us, mun, before you invited us to watch you die.

OSCAR begins singing the choral opening to "Hyacinth House" by The Doors. It is earnest and ridiculous.

OSCAR: Dididididum, dim dididim dim di di dum dum

Dididididum, dim dididim dim di di dum dum

PAM: Are you alright, Oscar?

OSCAR: Dididididum, dim dididim dim di di dum dum.

BRENDA: Please tell me he's not having a stroke and all.

Choral introduction complete, OSCAR now launches into the lyrics of "Hyacinth House".

BRENDA: Look at him, he's in his bloody garden in his head now. Thinks we're bloody flowers.

OSCAR sings the lyrics with its repetition about needing new friends.

MARGARET: I just need an aspirin.

BRENDA: You can't sing Edward happy, Oscar.

OSCAR: I can try.

He continues to sing.

PAM reaches out and touches OSCAR. He stops.

PAM: He's in pain, Oscar.

GEORGE: So am I with this singing.

PAM: You can try all you like but you can't take it away. And you can't ask them to pretend otherwise. It was the same with my mother.

ELIZABETH has walked up to THE NURSE.

ELIZABETH: Are you happy about this?

THE NURSE: Me?

ELIZABETH: Who else? This sits well with you? Playing God?

JAMES: I don't think you can start blaming her, Aunty.

ELIZABETH: How do we even know Edward is saying what she says he is?

PETER: I hadn't thought of that.

BRENDA: Far as I can see, he's lost his voice, not his wits. Reckon we'd know if she was making it all up like Margaret was.

MARGARET: I wasn't making it up. I was/

ELIZABETH: Maybe it's her idea then. What's she been whispering into my brother's ear?

MARGARET: *(To THE NURSE.)* What have you been saying to Edward?

ELIZABETH: Worming your way into our family, making Edward think terrible things.

JAMES: What has she been saying, Dad?

MARGARET: *(To EDWARD.)* Just because she understands you doesn't mean you should trust her.

ELIZABETH: Standing there as if butter wouldn't melt.

JAMES: Does anybody even know her name?

GIOVANNI: I do. I know her name.

MARGARET: Well bully for you.

OSCAR: *(About GIOVANNI.)* That fella seems to know what's what, doesn't he?

GIOVANNI: I know because I asked her.

THE NURSE: My name is Lucy. And it's true that none of you knows anything about me. I should think that was reason enough not to gang up on me, to attack me. It's not my place to bring myself, my personality, into this room. I pride myself on working quietly and unobtrusively.

261

ELIZABETH: You're toxic. Dishing out death when it's your job to help him live.

THE NURSE: Nursing isn't as simple as that.

ELIZABETH: Don't you talk to me about nursing. I know nursing.

THE NURSE: So do I. It's all I've ever done.

There are lots of parts to my job. Your brother is in pain.

ELIZABETH: He doesn't even know what pain is.

JAMES: How can you say that, Aunty?

ELIZABETH: Because I know. I know what pain is.

GEORGE: Where's this coming from, Elizabeth?

ELIZABETH takes in the room, makes a decision. Now is the time to share something she has never shared. When ELIZABETH starts, nothing can stop her and GEORGE's lines are layered over the top of her words, rather interruptions.

ELIZABETH: Pain is waiting for years to get pregnant, wishing, hoping, dreaming while your friends have child after child like it's easy.

GEORGE: What are you saying?

ELIZABETH: Pain is stretching your skin to grow your miracle baby in your womb for eight months and then being told he hasn't made it.

GEORGE: We didn't... I don't remember.

ELIZABETH: His heartbeat is nowhere to be found.

GEORGE: Oh.

ELIZABETH: Pain is longer and longer contractions without relief.

262

GEORGE: Oh.

ELIZABETH: When you know the baby in your womb is already dead.

GEORGE: Oh.

GEORGE remembers now.

GEORGE (CONT'D): Yes, I…

ELIZABETH: Pain is pushing and pushing, until your skin is torn and raw, to force out a baby who will never take a breath.

GEORGE: No. I can't bear it.

ELIZABETH: Pain is having that blue-lipped little boy pulled from your arms when all you want to do is clutch him to you and curl up and die with him.

GEORGE makes a guttural sound of pain.

ELIZABETH (CONT'D): Pain is when your husband tells you that you can't do that. You don't get to choose. You have to go on living and the only way to do that is to pretend it never happened. And you do that for years knowing that you're both carrying the pain of it. But then he starts to forget and all that pain rises up again because now you're carrying it alone.

GEORGE: *(Ashamed of himself for forgetting.)* How could I forget that? Our little boy.

ELIZABETH caresses GEORGE's face.

ELIZABETH: It's ok, my love.

ELIZABETH turns her attention to EDWARD, confronts him.

ELIZABETH (CONT'D): Pain, Edward? Pain? You don't know the meaning of the word. There are some things we get to choose in life and some we don't. We don't get to choose how we are born, how we birth our babies or how we die.

EDWARD leans in to THE NURSE who translates.

THE NURSE: I would like it if we could all sit down and eat our meal now.

ELIZABETH lashes out and swipes EDWARD's barbiturates off the table. EDWARD tries to recover them from the floor but he can't reach. He looks to THE NURSE to help. She goes to pick them up until PETER pipes up...

PETER: I wouldn't do that. If you pass him those, you're assisting. We're all witnesses to it.

THE NURSE stops, stands leaving the medication on the floor. EDWARD tries hard to get them. Everybody watches. Eventually...

JAMES: Somebody help him.

GEORGE goes to help. ELIZABETH stops him.

ELIZABETH: Don't even think about it.

JAMES: Pam?

MORVEN: You can't ask her.

PETER: Morven's right. She could get into trouble.

EDWARD is getting more and more distressed. He can't pick up the medication.

JAMES: Somebody help him.

ELIZABETH: No! He mustn't be allowed to do this.

GIOVANNI goes to ELIZABETH.

GIOVANNI: You carry a lot of heartache, Signora. It is good to let it out. It will bring you peace. But you must not spit it out. You must breathe it out.

He puts his arm around her and guides her to her seat. ELIZABETH lets him.

MARGARET: Just help him, Pam. It's what you do, what you've always done.

Everybody looks to PAM, who feels terribly conflicted. She gets up but hesitates.

Eventually…

PAM: I'm sorry, I can't. I won't. I'm sorry Mr. Voss.

PAM goes to sit down, feels everybody's eyes on her.

PAM (CONT'D): Do you know none of you have said anything nice about my dress? Not one of you.

(To MARGARET.) I've met my replacement, Ma'am, and I don't wish to be rude but she looks nothing like me. So I don't really know how you can say you keep forgetting that I've stopped working for you. Because that feels a little… I'm not trying to criticise or… but that feels a little hurtful really. I am more than what I do for you. I'm more than a squirty bottle of Cif, a mop and furniture polish. I am a person. And I've always felt a part of this family. And I hoped that's why I was invited today.

Nobody knows quite how to respond to this outburst. EDWARD is still desperately trying to get hold of the medication.

EDWARD: *(Unintelligible.)* Help. Somebody. Please.

BRENDA steps in. She hands him the medication. He looks up at her, grateful. She sees everybody is staring at them.

BRENDA: We going to eat this dinner or what?

Blackout.

THE NURSE 2

Out of time and place.

The following is delivered deadpan by THE NURSE.

THE NURSE: It's a funny thing to hold a person's life in your hands. Funny. I've got doses wrong before. I gave a patient eight tablets every two hours when the doctor told me to give two every eight. Another time I was supposed to give one tablet every twelve hours but I gave twelve every hour. Worst muddle I ever got into though was when a doctor told me to prick a patient's boil.

THE NURSE surveys the room, deadpan in spite of the punchline until...

They say, "laughter is the best medicine" but actually morphine is.

"Did you take the patient's temperature, Nurse?"

"No. Is it missing?"

Still deadpan.

I nursed a young marine who'd had his leg blown off by an IRA bomb in Kent. He couldn't stop laughing. Laughed and laughed until he lost consciousness. Funny thing, pain.

EATING SUPPER

Everybody is seated at the table, eating their main course.

JULIA and JONATHAN have rejoined the group. Nobody speaks.

MARGARET's phone beeps. She reads her message.

MARGARET: Excuse me.

MARGARET exits. The others continue to eat. Eventually...

JULIA: Will you be killing yourself before or after dessert, Daddy? Only I know you've never had much of a sweet tooth.

JAMES: Julia...

JULIA: Perhaps you'll wait until after coffee?

OSCAR: Isn't coffee after a meal supposed to stop you falling asleep?

JULIA: Good point, Oscar. You might want to skip the coffee, Daddy.

GIOVANNI: Maybe a liqueur?

JULIA: Oh yes, what a good idea. An amorretto or a sloe gin.

BRENDA: I like a nice Baileys.

PAM: Yes and you used to help yourself to the bottle in Mr Voss's cabinet.

PETER: Shouldn't it be a whisky, since we're... here?

BRENDA: Once, I did that. You've a memory like an elephant you have, Pam.

GEORGE: Yes, a good single malt. A Drumguish perhaps.

PAM: You're a serpent.

MORVEN: Has to be Laphroaig if you're going with whisky.

BRENDA: Steady on, Pam.

GEORGE: Nonsense. Laphroaig is overrated.

PAM: Whispering things into my ear: I'm invisible, I'm a mug for being helpful.

MORVEN: As the only Scot around this table, I think you can let me be the judge of the best single malt.

PAM: It's different for you. You had children, you had a family of your own. I started working for Mr Voss and his first wife when I was fourteen years old.

OSCAR: I actually prefer an Irish whiskey myself.

PAM: And I… love them and I think in their own way, they love me.

MORVEN: You could be arrested for saying that in Scotland, Oscar.

PAM: And you egged me on until I let them down. Let Mr Voss down.

OSCAR: Didn't think the Scots were so over-sensitive.

PAM: All so you could score points.

BRENDA: No, mun. It was compassion, that's all.

A moment.

JONATHAN: Campari's lovely if you fancy a pink drink.

ELIZABETH: Oh, I love a Campari.

GIOVANNI: Limoncello is my favourite.

JAMES: Tia Maria?

MORVEN: That's coffee again though, isn't it?

THE NURSE : Or perhaps a glass of port?

EDWARD clangs his fork against the candlestick repeatedly until he has everybody's attention. He gestures to THE NURSE who leans in to interpret for him.

EDWARD: *(Unintelligible.)* Not pain. Voice. No voice. Not to be understood.

268

THE NURSE: It's not the pain. It's the voice. The lack of it. To not be able to speak, to make myself understood.

JAMES: But you've never used your voice, Dad. You devoted yourself to the only military career where being silent and invisible was actually in the job title - "The Silent Service". Commanding a vessel of men who have to whisper so as not to be detected/

MORVEN: The whispering's not actually true. Just a thing they did in Russian spy films.

JONATHAN: No it is true. The ocean's like a loud speaker. Amplifies every sound.

PAM: Mr Voss once told me you can hear everything clear as a bell down there. Men used to weep at the whale song.

JULIA: He told you that?

PAM : He used to talk to me as I polished. Used to say I was the only person in the house quieter than him.

GEORGE: We used to talk about politics together. You had such strong, well-informed opinions.

ELIZABETH: Not Edward. You've got muddled again, George.

GEORGE: No. I haven't Elizabeth. We had a blazing row about it once. He was for the miners. Thought it was rotten how they were being treated and I told him to speak out. All those people trying to be heard and him, a Commander in Her Majesty's Navy, wouldn't open his mouth to support them even though he was with them in his heart. He said it wasn't his place. You've never used your voice, Edward.

JAMES: If there was ever a man who could live without a voice, it's you.

EDWARD starts to speak, desperately. Doesn't wait for THE NURSE to interpret. He gets frustrated when nobody can understand him.

EDWARD : *(Unintelligible.)* Don't understand. A man. A man. Who. Who/

THE NURSE: Slow down. I can't hear you. Come on now. Breathe.

EDWARD tries again. THE NURSE translates.

EDWARD: *(Unintelligible.)* Man who speaks. Conscience. Wrong. Told loves his feelings. Been known. Man no voice, ok.

THE NURSE: A man who has spoken out when his conscience told him something was wrong, told his loved ones how he feels, let himself be known, that man could have his voice taken from him.

EDWARD: *(Unintelligible.)* Man whose wife kills. His silence. Children, look. Me stranger. Safer with staff than family. Silent as they worked. Man losing voice. Punished. Too far. Paradise on horizon when sealed hatch.

THE NURSE : But the man whose wife killed herself because of his silence, whose children look at him like a stranger, who felt safer in the company of his staff than he did his own family because they let him be silent as they worked around him. For that man losing his voice is a punishment too far. Like seeing paradise on the horizon when you've already sealed the hatch.

BRENDA: *(Genuinely moved.)* Like being invited for a slap up meal and being made too sad to swallow it.

JAMES goes to his father.

JAMES: I don't want you to suffer. I know what it's like to need something even though it hurts those around you.

When everybody's happiness and love seems dependent on you remaining somewhere you can't. You invited my ex-wife instead of my partner here today because you still haven't accepted who I am. I've never truly had your blessing. But you can have mine. If this is how you want to go, you have my blessing.

EDWARD clasps JAMES's hand and holds it to his own heart. ANUSHKA enters to clear the plates. EDWARD gets himself up and holds out his arms to her.

EDWARD: *(Unintelligible.)* Sophie. Come to me, my love.

ANUSHKA hears him and walks towards him. Confused as to what he wants with his arms outstretched, she goes to pass him the plates.

JAMES: No, no.

BRENDA: Oh, hell.

THE NURSE: No.

THE NURSE intercepts the plates. EDWARD continues to hold his arms out to ANUSHKA. She looks at him, intrigued, bemused but his need of her communicates itself to her. With real tenderness, she strokes his face. Then, abruptly, takes the plates from THE NURSE and exits. EDWARD holds his hand to the cheek that ANUSHKA caressed.

JAMES: It's not her, Dad.

JULIA: Mummy's dead. And you're wrong. It wasn't because of your silence. Mummy was the only person who never needed words from you. You were made for each other.

EDWARD leans in and whispers in JULIA's ear. It isn't clear whether she understands him. When he has said what he wants to say, he takes JULIA's face in his hands and kisses her on the forehead.

JULIA sits. JONATHAN clasps her hand in his.

EDWARD speaks to THE NURSE, who translates.

EDWARD: *(Unintelligible.)* Looked after me, life, Pam. Never let down.

THE NURSE: You've looked after me most of my life, Pam. You could never let me down.

PAM is affected by this.

EDWARD: *(Unintelligible.)* Elizabeth. Didn't know. Suffered. Should have. Sorry.

THE NURSE: Elizabeth, I didn't know how much you suffered. I should have asked. I'm sorry.

ELIZABETH is very moved by this. GEORGE has already forgotten the heartbreak of earlier…

GEORGE: What's he saying? When did you suffer? Have I missed something?

ELIZABETH: Nothing my love.

EDWARD: *(Unintelligible.)* Oscar, no sing. First rate gardener. Singing bloody awful.

THE NURSE: *(Interpreting for EDWARD.)* Oscar, please don't sing again. You're a first rate gardener but your singing's bloody awful.

MARGARET pulls ROGER into the room.

ROGER: I don't think this is the best idea, Margaret.

MARGARET: Well I do.

ROGER: Why don't I just wait for you outside?

MARGARET: Everybody, I'd like you to meet Roger. Roger this is my son, James, his wife and his boyfriend over there in the ridiculous shirt.

ROGER: Wife and boyfriend? Oh. Excellent. Well hello all.

PETER: The first shirt was better, wasn't it?

JAMES: There's really not much in it, Peter.

MARGARET: My sister in law, my step-daughter, their
 husbands, a couple of our cleaners/

BRENDA: We have got names, you know.

PAM: Pam. Hello.

MARGARET: Our gardener and... I don't really know who
 you are.

GIOVANNI: Giovanni.

MARGARET: Yes, but who are you?

JONATHAN: He's some sort of counsellor, isn't he? Edward's
 therapist?

ELIZABETH: Must be, he's very insightful.

OSCAR: A religious man, I thought. Some kind of minister.

BRENDA: Or a life coach?

GIOVANNI: I work behind the wheel.

MARGARET: What's that? A new form of therapy or...

GIOVANNI: Brum, brum.

MARGARET: Sorry?

GIOVANNI mimes driving a car.

MORVEN: He's driving, aren't you. I'm a bit of a whizz at
 Charades. Are you Edward's chauffeur?

GIOVANNI: Yes and no. I drive the taxi for Edward from the
 station to here.

JULIA: You mean you've never met him before today?

GIOVANNI: No. I did not have that pleasure before.

JULIA: Unbelievable! Have you heard this, Jonathan?

JONATHAN: Yes, that is a little...

OSCAR: I don't feel so bad for being here now.

MARGARET: Edward invited you in, knowing what he was going to tell us, what he was planning on doing?

ROGER: Margaret...

JONATHAN: It is a little perplexing.

GIOVANNI: We connected with our souls.

OSCAR: I wouldn't call Mr. Voss family but I've known him a fair bit longer than this geezer.

PETER: He invited a taxi driver but not me.

JAMES: I can't believe it.

GIOVANNI: Stop this. Listen to me!

All are silenced.

GIOVANNI (CONT'D): What is this look of scorn when you say "taxi driver". That is very wrong.

I have had seven different women in labour in my cab. I deliver them to the hospital so they can deliver a new life into the world. One little person was minutes from being born centimetres away from me. I have had a man propose marriage. Not to me. To his woman. I have had a couple agree to divorce while they sit behind me. I have seen a father punch his young son in the head because the little boy had left his rucksack on the side of the road. I have delivered a weeping man to the funeral of his childhood sweetheart. I have taken a couple to the hospital in order for them to turn off their daughter's life support.

I see the whole world from my taxi cab. Taxi driver has as much soul as a religious man or therapist. My taxi cab is a confessional. I see their lives, hear their stories and give them absolution. But what do I take? For me? For my soul? They pay their fares and I never see them again. I am a canary watching the world from inside his cage.

Your husband, Signora, is the first man to invite me into his life. I am indebted to him. Spiritually not financially. Because in fact, he has not yet paid his fare.

ROGER: Well, it's very nice to meet you anyway. Do you have a business card? Good taxi man is always useful to know.

GIOVANNI: I write it down on a napkin for you.

ROGER: Much obliged.

GIOVANNI: Does anybody have a pen?

ROGER: I might. Let me check.

BRENDA: I've got one in my handbag.

MARGARET: Roger.

PAM: I've got one here. Take mine.

MARGARET: Roger.

ROGER: Much obliged. Pam was it? What a lovely dress.

At last! PAM is delighted.

PAM: Oh, thank you!

MARGARET: Roger!

ROGER: What?

MARGARET: This is my husband, Edward.

ROGER: Oh yes. Oh dear. Of course. Right. Hello Edward.

MARGARET: Edward, everything about tonight has been designed to humiliate me.

ROGER: Margaret, can I just have a quiet word?

MARGARET: From your choice of guests through to your decision not to inform me of your intentions privately.

ROGER: You don't need to do this.

MARGARET: Telling a taxi driver before your own wife, for example.

ROGER: There's really no need/

MARGARET: So while I can't imagine this is what you pictured for your… what are we calling this? A death party? A living wake?

ROGER: I'm really not very comfortable about/ this.

MARGARET: I won't apologise for bringing Roger here even though you may feel inadvertently as humiliated as I have this whole evening.

ROGER: Margaret, please.

MARGARET: Roger is my lover.

ROGER: Christ on a bike.

OSCAR: Crikey.

GEORGE: What did she say?

ELIZABETH: Shh.

JAMES: Mum?

JULIA: How could you?

MORVEN: I had my suspicions. I'm very sensitive about these things.

BRENDA: This is better than watching "The Valleys", this is.

MARGARET: Well? Do you have anything you'd like to say? If your Nurse would be kind enough to interpret your dribbling raspy excuse for a voice.

EDWARD whispers to THE NURSE, not taking his eyes off MARGARET.

MARGARET: Well?

All eyes on THE NURSE.

THE NURSE: No, I can't repeat that. I'm sorry. There are limits.

ROGER: Look, Edward, I… By the sounds of it, tonight's a pretty emotional night and I don't know what you're planning or… and it's none of my business. I'd just like to say…I didn't know she was married when…well I did but… When we first. NO, I knew. I can't pretend I didn't. I've no excuse really. This is terribly embarrassing and I feel. I mean, what a way to… Just terrible behaviour. What must you think of me? Hate me, I'll bet. You should. All of you. I do. It's just…

I like her hands. I like the grooves in the skin on her knuckles and the way the top of her little finger leans into her ring finger, like it's tired and wants a rest. I like her hair. I like to burrow my face into it. Her ear lobes are… perfection. I like her voice, it's so rich and full of her. And her eyes.

There's more life in her eyes than I've seen in a hundred people. And her mouth is… She tastes… But you don't want to know that. And her feet. They're not particularly lovely feet and yet I seem to….Every inch of her really.

I'm mad for her. I'm so sorry. And then again, I'm not because I'd follow her into a volcano if she wanted me to. I'd sink down to the centre of the earth with my skin being singed off, all to keep looking into those eyes.

I love her.

MARGARET: Bloody hell, Roger.

A silence. EDWARD speaks and THE NURSE interprets.

EDWARD: *(Unintelligible.)* Man. Man has. Fine voice.

THE NURSE: This man… has a fine voice.

JONATHAN: Bravo!

OSCAR: He's certainly got a way with words.

PAM: Such passion.

BRENDA: Steady on, Pam. You're all a quiver.

JONATHAN: How wonderful to bear your soul like that. To be totally open.

MORVEN: I could sense his passion the moment he walked in the room. I'm very sensitive about/

JULIA: You were married to James for twenty five years and didn't know he was gay, you're not that bloody sensitive, Morven.

MARGARET: Roger, that was/

ROGER: It just bubbled up. Sorry.

MARGARET: Don't be.

JONATHAN is on a mission. He makes his way to MARGARET's vanity case, opens it and rummages for a moment. JULIA sees him.

JULIA: Jonathan, now is not the time.

JONATHAN: Now is exactly the time. To say the things that should have been said before. To be the people we really are.

Please, Julia.

JULIA: Oh, alright.

JONATHAN rummages some more and when he emerges, he is wearing rouge and earrings. He swipes BRENDA's heels and ELIZABETH's shawl and walks slowly and elegantly back to his seat, kissing JULIA on the cheek.

JULIA (CONT'D): You look lovely, Darling.

JONATHAN: Thank you.

BRENDA: Are they my shoes?

JONATHAN: Yes, do you mind?

BRENDA: You're welcome to them – they hurt like hell.

GEORGE: What on earth's going on?

ELIZABETH: I've no idea.

ROGER: You didn't tell me your family were so… interesting, Margaret.

JONATHAN: Julia wanted me to come as Jonathan today. But I wanted you all to meet me properly. I'm Jonie. I've known I was in the wrong body since I was five years old and forced to play cricket with the boys. I hate cricket. I've always known. Not just about the cricket, of course. I was just too terrified to say the words until eighteen months ago.

MORVEN: Do you know, I always sensed there was something feminine about you, Jonathan.

JONATHAN: Well, you are very sensitive about these things, darling.

MORVEN: It's true.

JONATHAN: My wonderful wife has agreed to me transitioning so that my body will finally match my brain. Haven't you Julia?

JULIA: We can't both be cross and disappointed. We'd have no friends at all. I need you happy, my love. It brightens my world when you are.

JONATHAN: Your daughter is a remarkable woman, Edward.

EDWARD suddenly slumps in his chair. The empty bottle of Nembutal rolls out of his hand and across the floor.

JAMES: Dad?

PETER: Oh bloody hell.

JULIA: He took it?

MORVEN: He must have.

JONATHAN: Oh dear.

OSCAR: Crikey.

BRENDA: Oh mun.

PAM: Is he?

ROGER: Clear a space for him. Lie him down.

They lie EDWARD on the floor, everybody crowds round him. THE NURSE is checking his pulse.

ELIZABETH: Oh Edward, how could you?

GEORGE: What's happening?

GIOVANNI: Godspeed you, Signor Edward.

MARGARET: Edward? Edward, don't leave us. Please.

ROGER: Let the man have some air!

Everything suddenly pauses. Totally still.

THE DANCE

Out of time and place.

EDWARD rises from the floor, his family remain gathered round his horizontal "body". This is a strange sensation for EDWARD, free of his tired body. He enjoys it for a moment and then… ANUSHKA emerges. Only it isn't ANUSHKA. It's SOPHIE, his beloved first wife. They move towards each other like magnets drawn together. When their hands touch, they light up and begin a beautiful dance together. It is tender and playful and everything we could hope for a dying man to experience at the moment of his death.

When the dance is done, SOPHIE fades away. EDWARD melts back into his position lying on the floor. And click, we're back in the room.

AFTER

Everybody is gathered round EDWARD's body. THE NURSE is checking his pulse. She lets go of his wrist.

THE NURSE : He's gone. I'm sorry.

JULIA: Daddy!

JULIA is comforted by JONATHAN.

JAMES: Oh God.

In his distress, JAMES turns towards MORVEN and weeps.

MORVEN: I'm here, my love. Morven's here.

ROGER: Oh Margaret, I'm so sorry.

MARGARET: Just hold me.

BRENDA: Are you crying?

PAM: No.

BRENDA: Well I bloody am. Give us a cwtch will you.

PAM and BRENDA hug.

ELIZABETH: Edward, you stubborn fool.

GEORGE: Let him go, Elizabeth. Let him go.

GIOVANNI: *(To OSCAR.)* In Italia a man can hug a man if they feel a big emotion like this. We can hug if you would like.

OSCAR: We don't do that here, no.

PETER watches JAMES being held by MORVEN and feels redundant and hurt. He backs out of the room.

MORVEN: There, there. I'm here. This is exactly why your father invited me. He knew you would need me now.

JAMES recovers himself enough to realise who he has turned to. It doesn't feel right.

JAMES: But I don't want you. I want Peter. Where's my Peter?

PETER hears just in time and stays. JAMES rushes to him and they hold each other.

THE NURSE: Goodbye Edward.

THE NURSE kisses EDWARD tenderly. GIOVANNI goes to THE NURSE.

GIOVANNI: You gave him a voice, Lucy. A beautiful voice.

THE NURSE nods, visibly moved. GIOVANNI comforts her with a hug, which she accepts gladly.

GEORGE: He's given the order and he's diving down now. Deeper and deeper into dark water. A Commander goes down with his vessel and Edward's at peace down there listening to the music of the ocean. We mustn't pity him.

Oscar starts to sing Stevie Wonder's "Come Back As A Flower".

ANUSHKA enters, ignoring the room, the tears and hugs of consolation, EDWARD lying on the floor. She places a tray of dessert on the table unceremoniously and goes to exit. She stops when she sees EDWARD, looks at him for a moment, then looks up at the room.

ANUSHKA: He not want lem-on mi-rang pie?

Blackout.

End.

OF BLOOD
by Christopher William Hill

All rights whatsoever in this play are strictly reserved and application for performance etc. should be made before rehearsal to MBA Literary Agents Ltd, 62 Grafton Way, London W1T 5DW. No performance may be given unless a licence has been obtained.

Characters

Female	*Male*
COUNTESS	GYORGY
KATALIN	VIDOR
ZSOFI	KRISTOF
ILKA	MATYAS
AGOTHA	RUDI
TEREZ	DOG
VIRAG	COOK
NURSE	GABOR

Of Blood was first performed in the GBS Theatre at RADA on Friday 14 December 2018.

DIRECTOR – Vivian Munn
WRITER – Christopher William Hill
DESIGNER – Miguel Guzman
MOVEMENT TUTOR – Angela Gasparetto
VOICE TUTOR – Caroline Kilpatrick

Cast
COUNTESS – Jo Cooklin
KATALIN – Sara Carroll
ZSOFI – Bruna Cattini
ILKA – Paulette McLatchie
AGOTHA – Catherine Herman
TEREZ – Linda Jennings
VIRAG – Ags Irwin
NURSE – Vicki Edmunds
GYORGY – John Northeast
VIDOR – Drew Paterson
KRISTOF – Andrew Shepherd
MATYAS – Charles Molloy
RUDI – Jim Mulligan
DOG – Marek Urbanowicz
COOK – Keith Biley
GABOR – Neville Price
*Due to the indisposition of Martin Doolan special thanks goes to Jim Mulligan

Production Team
STAGE MANAGER – Zarah Cooper
DEPUTY STAGE MANAGER – Cassidy Davis
LIGHTING DESIGNER & OPERATOR – Lucía Sánchez Roldán
SOUND DESIGNER & OPERATOR – Henry Boothroyd
COSTUME SUPERVISOR – Hannah Driver

SCENE ONE

The panelled walls of an ancient castle chamber. Dogs bark, off. RUDI, a horseman, enters – he wears a long riding cape. An old woman, NURSE, enters.

NURSE: We'd given you up for lost.

There is a rustle in the shadows and a voice speaks softly.

COUNTESS: Where have you been?

RUDI: Three days from here.

COUNTESS: You came through the forest?

RUDI: Yes. Down from the mountains and on through the forest. It was hard going… the earth was churned up. The carriage juddered up over the rocks and the axle broke… so we made our way by foot through the bracken. There were wolves at our heels –

COUNTESS: But what have you brought me?

RUDI smiles.

RUDI: There's more than wolves among the trees.

He reveals a small baby from inside his coat.

COUNTESS: A child?

She pulls further back into the shadows. RUDI holds out the baby to the NURSE.

RUDI: Take her.

NURSE steps forward.

NURSE: Oh, my prettiness!

She takes the baby and holds it to her breast, rocking it gently. The baby gurgles.

Baby's got a hunger.

She reaches inside her clothing.

The teat's gone dry.

The baby cries.

Shh… shh. No need to cry.

She holds the baby tighter.

There'll be milk running soon enough.

She lowers her voice.

Bite and suck… you'll get the habit of it.

She rocks the baby, then an animal look overcomes her. Beat. Ducking out of RUDI's way, the NURSE runs off with the baby.

COUNTESS: No… stop her…

RUDI pursues NURSE off. A baby's cry seems to echo around the castle walls. Then silence. RUDI returns, his face smeared with blood.

Where is the child?

RUDI: Gone, Mistress.

COUNTESS: Gone?

RUDI: Taken.

The COUNTESS cries out in the darkness.

SCENE TWO

Time has passed. Three ladies-in-waiting lean out from the windows of the castle.

AGOTHA: What can you see now?

ILKA: My eyes have gone.

ZSOFI: Pity your ears haven't.

AGOTHA: There's wheels turning… churning up the mud.

ZSOFI: A carriage!

AGOTHA: A woman.

> *RUDI, enters, with a woman – KATALIN. She is simply dressed in hat, coat and gloves – she has a travelling case with her.*

RUDI: Dog!

> *DOG approaches.*

Put the horses to feed.

> *DOG nods and hurries off.*

KATALIN: Are there wolves in the forest?

RUDI: There are.

KATALIN: Have you seen them?

RUDI: Seen them. Been bit by them. Bit back.

KATALIN: How deep is the forest?

RUDI: Deep enough.

> *Beat.*

You'd starve among the trees before you could ever find your way out again.

> *The horses whinny and stamp, off.*

KATALIN: What's wrong with the beasts?

RUDI: They want water.

> *He exits, calling.*

Dog!

His voice is met by an answering howl. GABOR climbs through a small door with a large bundle of keys.

GABOR: You're here at last.

KATALIN: You were expecting me?

GABOR grunts – he unlocks the gate and pushes it open. KATALIN does not move.

GABOR: You want to freeze out there? Come.

He leads KATALIN through the gates, pushing them closed behind her.

SCENE THREE

KATALIN enters the castle and slowly pulls off her gloves. She stands in a pitch-dark passageway. There are whispers in the shadows. GABOR hurries past with his keys...

KATALIN: Where am I to go?

... but GABOR steps through a small door and is gone. VIDOR, a butler, approaches – he carries a lantern.

VIDOR: You are the girl.

KATALIN does not know how to reply. VIDOR beckons for her to follow him – the ladies-in-waiting laugh in the darkness.

You'll be tired.

KATALIN: Yes.

VIDOR: And hungry?

KATALIN: Is there bread and cheese?

VIDOR: That's peasant food.

KATALIN: I am a peasant.

VIDOR holds out the lantern, revealing ILKA standing silently in the shadows.

VIDOR: You heard.

ILKA nods.

Get food for the child.

KATALIN: Child?

She lets out an involuntary laugh and VIDOR turns sharply with the lantern.

VIDOR: I will take you to your chamber.

He holds out the lantern as before and ILKA has now vanished. VIDOR guides KATALIN along the passageway.

KATALIN: It's dark here.

VIDOR: The shutters are kept closed. Flies gather at the windows.

KATALIN: I was taught that flies are lost souls… beating their wings against the glass as they try to escape.

VIDOR: That's just superstition.

KATALIN: Yes.

VIDOR walks on along the passageway.

VIDOR: There's no such thing as a soul.

KATALIN is left in darkness – she hurries to catch up.

SCENE FOUR

KATALIN's chamber, morning. KATALIN pulls back the shutters and leans out of the window. The ladies-in-waiting enter the room. ZSOFI carries a jug of water. ILKA hisses to AGOTHA.

ILKA: The window!

AGOTHA shoves KATALIN to one side. She closes the window and shutters it.

AGOTHA: The shutters stay closed.

ILKA: Weren't you told?

ZSOFI: There's water to wash with.

KATALIN: Thank you.

ZSOFI sets the jug down beside a basin.

ZSOFI: How did you sleep?

AGOTHA: Did you sleep?

KATALIN: I slept like the dead.

AGOTHA laughs and ILKA hits her.

AGOTHA: Where do you come from?

KATALIN: From the mountains.

She pours water from the jug into the basin – she dips her fingers.

The water's cold.

ZSOFI: It's a long walk from the kitchens.

Beat. KATALIN washes her face in the basin.

KATALIN: Are there prayers?

ZSOFI: Not here.

AGOTHA: I pray to die sometimes.

ILKA: Ignore her.

ZSOFI: Arms.

KATALIN: What?

ZSOFI: Hold your arms out.

Obstinately, KATALIN crosses her arms behind her back.

KATALIN: If there are no prayers what do I do?

ILKA: Do what you like.

AGOTHA: She won't care.

KATALIN: Who won't?

AGOTHA: *She* won't.

ZSOFI: Arms!

KATALIN finally holds out her arms. ZSOFI pulls off KATALIN's outer clothing – KATALIN gasps and clutches her left arm.

ILKA: What's that…

AGOTHA: … on your arm?

KATALIN: It's nothing. It's a graze.

She licks the blood from her grazed arm.

See?

The ladies-in-waiting watch, spellbound. A bell rings out breaking the moment.

ZSOFI: Go…

ILKA and AGOTHA hurry away. ZSOFI turns to KATALIN.

Call if you need me.

She exits as KATALIN washes herself.

SCENE FIVE

Outside in the courtyard, washing has been hung out from ropes. Pigs grunt nearby. KATALIN walks outside – she smiles, weaving in and out of the drying laundry. She suddenly collides with a man, GYORGY, who enters with a wooden pail.

KATALIN: Watch where you're going!

GYORGY doesn't reply.

Do you know who I am?

GYORGY: Yes.

KATALIN: Then tell me.

She smiles.

I don't know who I am here.

TEREZ: *(Off, laughing.)* Gyorgy… Gyorgy…

She enters – but stops, watching KATALIN closely.

GYORGY: This is Terez…

VIRAG enters with clean laundry.

… that's Virag,

The women bow to KATALIN.

KATALIN: You don't need to bow.

Beat.

VIRAG: It's not through choice.

KATALIN: Why is everyone old here?

She laughs.

I never wanted to live beyond sixty.

GYORGY: What happened?

KATALIN: I turned sixty.

NURSE enters, a baby wrapped up in her arms. The women whisper among themselves.

NURSE: You're new.

She rocks the baby gently.

KATALIN: You've got a baby.

NURSE nods.

Show me.

NURSE: No.

KATALIN takes a step forward. NURSE shouts.

No!

She hushes the baby.

Mustn't scare baby.

She holds her finger to her lips and smiles. She rocks the baby gently in her arms.

You ever had the feel of a baby up against your tit?

KATALIN does not reply.

No feeling like it. Better than the kiss of a man... it's gentle and loving.

She gasps.

Not so hard now, little one...

She tries gently to push the baby away.

… I told you…

She rocks the baby harder.

… little teeth like needles tearing through the gums…

She winces with pain.

Curse you!

She cries out and throws the baby into the air – it falls to the ground, revealing nothing more than a bundle of clothes. She stands still, laughing. ZSOFI enters, drying her hands in her apron.

ZSOFI: What are you doing out?

NURSE stares blankly at her. ZSOFI gathers up the clothes and tucks them back into NURSE's arms.

NURSE: She's sleeping.

ZSOFI: Yes.

The NURSE rocks the baby gently as ZSOFI leads her off.

I'll take you back inside.

KATALIN: What's wrong with her?

GYORGY: It's play-acting to entertain the bitch.

KATALIN: What do you mean?

GYORGY: She likes to have a baby in this place.

KATALIN: Why?

GYORGY shrugs. He bangs a spoon against the pail and the pigs grunt in response. He feeds the pigs, scattering food on the ground. He claps his hands together and the pigs snort.

GYORGY: Don't trust a thing she says to you.

A bell rings loudly. KATALIN smiles at GYORGY and exits.

TEREZ: I've seen the way you look at her.

GYORGY: What do you mean?

VIRAG laughs.

I don't look at her like anything.

The bell rings again.

TEREZ: What are you waiting for? The old hag wants you.

GYORGY turns – he empties out the last of the pig feed and exits.

SCENE SIX

The COUNTESS's chamber. The COUNTESS sits on a throne-like seat, DOG is curled up at her feet. The ladies-in-waiting are in attendance. There are tazzas of sweetmeats on a side table – marzipan and figs stuffed with almonds.

COUNTESS: What is she like?

She reaches down to tickle DOG's ear.

ILKA: Very plain.

COUNTESS: Bring her to me.

ILKA: Yes, Mistress.

She exits and returns with KATALIN.

Stand upright.

KATALIN straightens her back.

COUNTESS: Leave us.

The ladies-in-waiting back away. The COUNTESS points to ILKA.

Not you.

DOG raises his head.

Or you.

DOG settles down again. ILKA stays as ZSOFI and AGOTHA exit.

What do they call you, child?

KATALIN: Nobody calls me anything anymore.

COUNTESS: Come here… come to me.

KATALIN walks slowly towards the COUNTESS and gives a low bow.

That will do, girl. Stand up. Stand.

KATALIN stands.

Let me look at you.

She beckons to KATALIN who steps forward.

Closer.

KATALIN takes another step forward.

Turn for me.

KATALIN turns.

You've got a good figure.

KATALIN: Yes.

COUNTESS: Let me kiss you.

KATALIN inclines her head and the COUNTESS kisses her on the cheek. DOG sniffs at KATALIN's skirts.

ILKA: *(Low.)* Down, dog.

'The COUNTESS holds her hand to KATALIN's face and slowly brushes it across her cheek.

COUNTESS: You're cold like marble.

ILKA: Make up the fire, dog.

DOG whines.

COUNTESS: Do as you're told.

DOG gets up from the floor and crosses to the fireplace.

COUNTESS: How was your journey here?

KATALIN: Hard. The roads were pitted and the carriage rocked me till my bones rattled. I heaved my guts so many times I thought I'd be vomited inside-out.

DOG laughs and ILKA kicks him.

COUNTESS: You came from far away?

KATALIN: A village in the mountains.

COUNTESS: Will you miss it?

KATALIN: It was a backwards place. They believed all sorts there.

Beat.

But the air was good.

COUNTESS: What did they believe?

KATALIN: They worshipped God but they kept their fingers crossed. When your man came with the carriage… all the plaster saints in the church had been turned to face the walls.

She laughs.

They're superstitious there.

She looks around.

It's dark here.

COUNTESS: I like it that way.

KATALIN: Is there ever sun?

301

DOG whines.

COUNTESS: Is your room comfortable?

KATALIN: Yes.

COUNTESS: Have you been well fed?

KATALIN: Yes.

She stops beside the table of sweetmeats.

COUNTESS: I am to teach you here.

KATALIN: That's what I was told.

COUNTESS: Do you know poetry?

KATALIN: I don't.

COUNTESS: Do you know your languages… French? German? Do you know English?

KATALIN: No.

ILKA laughs.

ILKA: What do you know?

KATALIN: I know not to ask questions.

She reaches her hand out slowly and takes two stuffed figs from one of the tazzas.

It was good of you to take me in.

She eats one fig and tucks the other into a pocket.

COUNTESS: You were alone.

KATALIN: Yes.

COUNTESS: Were you never married?

KATALIN: No one wanted me.

COUNTESS: I'm sure that wasn't true.

KATALIN: It was.

Beat.

I never wanted a husband anyway. Some bear of a man wanting me to cook and clean for him and bring him sons. Never liked the thought of standing at the altar, with flowers twisted into my hair... and the priest... stinking of brandy and sin...

She stops and looks around. ILKA and DOG are staring at her.

Everybody watches me here.

COUNTESS: Does that disturb you?

KATALIN: No.

She eats another fig and bows to ILKA and DOG.

I like to be watched.

The COUNTESS smiles.

COUNTESS: What else do you like?

KATALIN: I like figs stuffed with almonds.

Beat.

There's a smell here.

COUNTESS: Old wood.

KATALIN: Maybe.

SCENE SEVEN

The ladies-in-waiting attend to the COUNTESS's makeup, whitening her face. Her wig has been removed and is being dressed by ZSOFI on a wig block. The COUNTESS scratches at her head.

ILKA: Don't scratch.

COUNTESS: It itches.

ILKA: It itches because you scratch at it.

The ladies-in-waiting lower the wig onto the COUNTESS's head.

Stop fidgeting.

The ladies-in-waiting fit the wig.

AGOTHA: Eyes closed.

The COUNTESS closes her eyes as ILKA blows powder onto the wig.

Do you see pretty things in your head, Mistress?

The COUNTESS reaches for AGOTHA's arm, squeezing it so hard that she cries out in pain.

COUNTESS: Do you?

ZSOFI fastens a string of pearls around the COUNTESS's neck. ILKA takes a small gilt box from the folds of her skirts and glues a sparkling patch to the COUNTESS's cheek.

COUNTESS: So much work to achieve so little.

ILKA: I'm not a miracle worker.

AGOTHA: Miracles are in short supply.

ILKA: Who asked you?

AGOTHA snaps her teeth at ILKA.

COUNTESS: Stop bickering.

The ladies-in-waiting crowd around her, fussing with her clothes and jewellery.

Don't fuss around me.

She stands as a dinner gong sounds.

SCENE EIGHT

The clock chimes as the COUNTESS and KATALIN enter the dining room. VIDOR and GABOR pull back the chairs and the COUNTESS and KATALIN sit at either end of the table. Servants enter with dishes and stand alongside the table. VIDOR claps his hands. The serving covers are removed and the plates of food are laid on the table.

COUNTESS: Venison.

She nods, approvingly.

VIDOR: Countess?

COUNTESS: Carve, Vidor.

VIDOR bows and carves the meat. He offers the meat but KATALIN pushes her plate away.

Aren't you hungry?

KATALIN: There's nothing here that I like.

COUNTESS: Take them away.

VIDOR: But Countess –

The COUNTESS turns her head sharply and VIDOR claps his hands. The servants return the covers to the serving dishes and exit.

COUNTESS: Wine.

VIDOR fills her glass. KATALIN smiles and holds out her glass, which VIDOR fills.

305

What do you like to eat?

KATALIN: I liked the food in the mountains.

To VIDOR.

The peasant food.

COUNTESS: What food did you eat there?

KATALIN: Plain food. Maize porridge for breakfast. Curd cheese.

COUNTESS: And for dinner?

KATALIN: There was paprika chicken for dinner.

COUNTESS: Were there dumplings too?

KATALIN: If I made them.

Pause.

COUNTESS: What are they eating in the kitchens?

VIDOR: It's common food.

COUNTESS: Tell me.

VIDOR: Chicken broth and rye bread.

COUNTESS: Then bring it to us. Now.

VIDOR bows and exits.

Do you miss the mountains?

KATALIN: I miss the food. Not the people. They said bad things about me.

COUNTESS: What did they say?

KATALIN: Things I can never repeat, they're so wicked.

COUNTESS: You think I'll be shocked?

KATALIN: We had coarse ways in the mountains.

Beat.

COUNTESS: Tell me.

KATALIN stands and walks slowly around the table.

KATALIN: They said I killed my child.

Beat.

What do you think of that?

COUNTESS: You said you were never married.

KATALIN: There's more than one way to get a baby.

SCENE NINE

The kitchens of the castle – a hive of activity. GYORGY, KRISTOF and RUDI drink from tankards. COOK and MATYAS pound dough at a table. TEREZ and VIRAG prepare broth at an ancient stove. DOG gnaws at a meat bone.

COOK: She turned the food away?

KRISTOF: She did.

He pours ale into his tankard.

COOK: Never known food to be turned away here.

GYORGY: She knows her own mind.

TEREZ stares at him.

KRISTOF: It's not her mind that interests me.

COOK: No?

KRISTOF takes a gulp of his ale.

KRISTOF: I'm hard for her.

VIRAG laughs.

I've been hard.

VIRAG: You were never hard. Not now... not even then.

MATYAS: Some doughs take longer to rise than others.

VIRAG laughs again – and TEREZ smiles in spite of herself.

VIRAG: And some dough never rises.

The women laugh.

What do you think, Terez?

TEREZ: Me?

She watches GYORGY.

All I want is enough stirring in his breeches to stir the heart.

VIRAG: It's always heart with you.

TEREZ: What's wrong with that?

VIRAG: Nothing.

TEREZ stirs the pot.

TEREZ: I don't see what there is to like about the girl.

KRISTOF: Don't you?

TEREZ: I never do with mountain girls. Their white faces and the smell of milk about them.

DOG howls.

KRISTOF: Hold your tongue, dog!

DOG growls and KRISTOF raises his hand.

TEREZ: Leave the creature alone, Kristof.

DOG turns away, yapping quietly to himself. He nuzzles up against TEREZ. KRISTOF pours out more ale.

MATYAS: There can't be a virgin within fifty miles of this place.

COOK: Man or woman.

RUDI: I'd settle for either.

MATYAS: You'd think there were no virgins nowhere these days.

He lifts the tankard to his lips.

I know there's none here!

SCENE TEN

The COUNTESS is asleep on her throne. The ladies-in-waiting stand uncertainly round the chair. ZSOFI holds a syringe in her hands. AGOTHA leans in and the COUNTESS opens her eyes suddenly. AGOTHA gasps.

ILKA: Mistress, we didn't mean to –

COUNTESS: I was awake.

AGOTHA sniggers.

AGOTHA: Thought you were a corpse.

Beat.

We were ready to lay you out in your grave clothes.

ILKA jabs AGOTHA in the ribs.

ILKA: Hold your tongue.

AGOTHA: Bitch.

She pushes back and ILKA knocks against ZSOFI, who pricks her finger on the syringe. The COUNTESS watches as ZSOFI sucks her thumb.

COUNTESS: Is there blood?

ZSOFI nods. The women are suddenly distracted but attempt to go about their business.

ILKA curtsies to the COUNTESS.

ILKA: Is there anything we can get you, Mistress?

AGOTHA: A book to read?

ILKA: A puzzle to solve?

AGOTHA: A sweetmeat to savour?

ILKA: Savour?

AGOTHA: I like pretty words.

ILKA snorts.

COUNTESS: I want nothing.

ZSOFI: Nothing?

COUNTESS: Nothing.

ZSOFI goes to exit. The COUNTESS attempts to control her instincts, but –

Wait…

ZSOFI stops – she steps back into the room and holds out her hand to the COUNTESS, who sucks hard at the bleeding thumb. ZSOFI sighs.

ZSOFI: Have you had your fill?

COUNTESS: Never.

ZSOFI: I know what you're really hungry for and there's nothing I can do, Mistress.

COUNTESS: No.

She laughs. AGOTHA and ILKA moan.

Feed them.

ZSOFI: Mistress…

She turns to AGOTHA, who crawls forward and sucks ZSOFI's thumb – ILKA pushes her out of the way, and feeds hungrily. The COUNTESS climbs from her chair and sweeps from the room.

SCENE ELEVEN

The wind has whipped up and howls around the castle walls. KATALIN leans out from her window. GYORGY watches from below. KATALIN attempts to cry out – but her voice is lost against the wind. The wind becomes the cawing of a raven – a loud, almost nightmarish sound.

SCENE TWELVE

KRISTOF stands outside, in the apple orchard. He wears a leather gauntlet on his arm. The raven caws from high above. KRISTOF turns, watching the bird in flight. KATALIN enters, her shawl wrapped around her shoulders - she cranes her head to the sky.

KRISTOF: You like my bird?

KATALIN: Is it a raven?

KRISTOF: It is.

He holds up a piece of meat and catches the bird on his arm.

You want to take him?

KATALIN nods. She binds her shawl around her arm as a gauntlet.

Ready?

KATALIN nods. KRISTOF passes the raven onto KATALIN's arm.

Don't show him that you're frightened.

KATALIN: I'm not.

She smiles and strokes the bird.

KRISTOF: Be gentle with him.

The raven caws and KATALIN cries out.

KATALIN: He pecks hard.

Beat.

Is he angry with me?

KRISTOF: Why? What've you done?

KATALIN stares at him. KRISTOF smiles.

You'll know when he's angry. He'll peck with that beak and twist.

He takes the raven back from KATALIN.

Ravens are clever creatures. They know how to cause the most pain.

He shakes his arm hard and watches as the raven takes to the sky. The raven cries out, high above – KATALIN watches. KRISTOF whistles for the bird. He holds out his arm and catches the raven as it lands.

KATALIN: Does he always return when you whistle?

KRISTOF: I've got him well trained.

Pause.

KATALIN: What if he didn't come back?

KRISTOF: He knows that if he didn't I'd come searching for him.

He strokes the bird.

And then I'd break his neck.

SCENE THIRTEEN

Outside in the yard, lit by moonlight. KATALIN enters with a bowl of slops. TEREZ and VIRAG enter.

KATALIN: It's cold tonight.

The women do not answer. KATALIN is amused by this.

Maybe you didn't hear... I said it's cold tonight.

TEREZ and VIRAG turn their backs.

Talk to me... don't talk.

She empties out the bowl.

I don't care much either way.

The women watch KATALIN as she crosses the yard.

TEREZ: Bitch.

KATALIN stops and turns.

KATALIN: What did you call me?

VIRAG: You heard.

TEREZ spits in KATALIN's face. KATALIN wipes away the spit.

TEREZ: Gyorgy is my man.

KATALIN: Your man? Then tell him, don't tell me.

VIRAG: You've got him bewitched.

KATALIN: Is that right?

TEREZ: I've seen...

KATALIN smiles.

... watched him watching you. Seen the magic working in your eyes.

KATALIN comes close to TEREZ.

KATALIN: There's no magic in your eyes. They're old... dead.

Beat.

Is it my fault if he stares at me? No. Is it my fault if I'm younger than you... more beautiful than you? No. It's just the way of things.

Beat.

When I've done with him I'll give him back.

Laughing, she stalks off.

SCENE FOURTEEN

Moonlight floods into KATALIN's chamber. Bells chime from a distant village. KATALIN stands close to the window, her back to the wall. ZSOFI enters.

ZSOFI: You should ring when it gets dark. That's what the bell is for.

KATALIN: I'm not used to having things done for me.

ZSOFI lights a taper.

I'm cold.

ZSOFI: That's what you get sitting at an open window.

She lights the candles with the taper.

KATALIN: My neck is stiff.

ZSOFI wraps the shawl around KATALIN's shoulders.

Thank you.

Without looking out, ZSOFI closes the shutters.

Aren't you curious?

Pause.

ZSOFI: I don't look out anymore.

KATALIN: Why not?

ZSOFI: What good will looking do me?

She fastens the shutters.

What good will it do any of us?

KATALIN: There's a house.

ZSOFI: Is that so?

KATALIN: Far off…

ZSOFI: Through the forest.

KATALIN: You know the place?

ZSOFI: I do. But no one lives there now.

KATALIN: How do you know?

ZSOFI: I know.

KATALIN: I saw smoke rising up from between the trees.

ZSOFI: It was mist. I told you… no one lives there. No fire… no smoke… just us and the trees.

KATALIN: In my head there's a family. A man and his wife… and children. They're sitting with chairs drawn up beside the fire. There's food on the table and –

ZSOFI: That's not what you see. That's what you *want* to see.

KATALIN: Does it matter?

ZSOFI: It matters. Don't you understand?

Beat.

It's not the same.

KATALIN: *(Wryly.)* Are you happy here?

ZSOFI stops and laughs.

ZSOFI: Happy?

KATALIN pulls the shawl tighter around her shoulders.

KATALIN: Have you always lived here?

ZSOFI: No.

KATALIN: How old were you when you came?

ZSOFI: I can't remember back so far.

She stops.

I was young... I remember that much. I was pretty...

She laughs.

... not pretty, but I was young. That was enough. There were fish in the river and deer in the forest. And people lived in the house in the trees.

KATALIN: What happened to them?

The bell rings, off. ZSOFI becomes serious again.

ZSOFI: I see nothing, I hear nothing, I know nothing.

SCENE FIFTEEN

VIRAG, TEREZ, MATYAS and COOK enter with stools and sit on stage. They mime the actions of plucking poultry.

COOK: Remember how it was?

VIRAG laughs.

VIRAG: I remember.

MATYAS: We all remember.

TEREZ: That's what pains.

COOK: Before dry-as-bone rituals… when blood ran freely.

VIRAG: I remember a girl came with her governess from one of the villages.

COOK: What girl?

MATYAS: Guileless thing.

COOK: Oh… that girl!

MATYAS: Where's the sport in a convent girl!

The servants laugh.

COOK: Bobbed the head as she came in under the gate…

TEREZ: … wouldn't turn eyes up to no man that greeted her.

MATYAS: Skin pale as buttermilk and crimson round the cheeks… the hour was late and the air cold enough to stop the heart.

COOK: Great slab of a woman the governess was.

MATYAS: She'd never wanted for meat, that one!

TEREZ: Had a taste for ale…

VIRAG: Ease itself to tempt the girl down to the kitchens…

COOK holds out his arms.

COOK: Run to my arms, little granddaughter.

They laugh.

VIRAG: Little granddaughter!

COOK: That's what I said.

MATYAS: Didn't know which way to turn.

COOK: Running this way… then that way…

They play out in mime the capture of the girl.

MATYAS: And the feathers were tossed up like a snowstorm.

VIRAG: She stumbled and she fell.

COOK: Scraped knees.

MATYAS: Pinched cheeks.

TEREZ: What a state the girl was in!

VIRAG flicks up the hem of her apron to fan the goose feathers.

VIRAG: Goosey down on her sticky face.

MATYAS: Come here, girl… I'll save you.

They laugh.

COOK: *(Whispered.)* He means you harm. Run to me, girly.

VIRAG: Beckoning her over.

MATYAS: Tearing at her clothes.

They cut at the girl with their knives.

VIRAG: No amount of book learning could prepare the girl for that.

COOK: Hot sticky breath crackling out of her.

They lower their knives.

TEREZ: She killed the girl for sport.

VIRAG: Things were better then.

Archly, MATYAS smacks his lips.

MATYAS: Youth is wasted on the old!

The servants hoot with laughter.

SCENE SIXTEEN

The castle solarium, the shutters closed. AGOTHA idly sweeps the floor with a broom. The COUNTESS enters the room with ILKA.

ILKA: What troubles you?

COUNTESS: Do you care?

ILKA: I don't care.

COUNTESS: Then why ask?

ILKA: Conversation falls into patterns.

AGOTHA stops brushing.

AGOTHA: You know what I'm thinking?

COUNTESS: There's not a thought in your head that I don't already know.

AGOTHA snorts and continues sweeping. KATALIN enters with a custard glass and spoon.

COUNTESS: Where have you been?

KATALIN: Why?

COUNTESS: Why?

Beat.

Because I asked you why.

KATALIN shifts uneasily.

KATALIN: To the kitchens.

Beat.

I was hungry.

COUNTESS: Hungry for what?

KATALIN does not reply.

AGOTHA: I'm always hungry.

COUNTESS: I've been hunting for you.

KATALIN: And now you've caught me.

She eats the custard, watched closely by AGOTHA.

What is this place?

ILKA: The solarium.

KATALIN: Even the solarium's shuttered against the sun!

She frowns at AGOTHA, pushing her foot through a mound of dust.

There's dirt on the floor.

AGOTHA: We sweep, we don't gather. Time passes faster than I can push a broom.

ILKA: If it falls it stays fallen.

AGOTHA smiles.

AGOTHA: There's custard on your chin.

She reaches out a finger. KATALIN wipes the custard away and licks her hand.

I like custard.

COUNTESS: It's not for you.

AGOTHA: Nothing's ever for me.

ILKA: The broom's for you. So sweep.

Cursing under her breath, AGOTHA continues to sweep the dust into a corner of the room.

SCENE SEVENTEEN

Outside, in the apple orchard. Birds sing. KATALIN lies back on the grass watching as the men fill baskets from the apple trees. KATALIN smiles at the men as they watch her. DOG enters and KATALIN sits up.

KATALIN: Dog… dog!

DOG takes a step forward.

Come and sit with me.

DOG approaches cautiously.

Don't be afraid.

DOG: I'm not.

KATALIN: Then come closer.

DOG crawls forward and KATALIN offers her hand to him. She makes a fuss of him and he rests his head in her lap, whining softly.

KATALIN: Were you always dog?

DOG: I've been many things. I was young dogsbody, then I was dogsbody, then for a time I was still dogsbody, then I was old dogsbody. Then I was dog. Still am dog.

KATALIN: That's quite a journey.

DOG: There's only dead dog left for dog.

KATALIN strokes his head.

KATALIN: I'd look after you.

DOG: I'm Mistress's dog.

KATALIN: Can't we share you?

DOG: Of all the dogs I've been I'm not a dog for sharing.

He bites KATALIN hard and she cries out. DOG scampers away.

Shake the apples from the trees! I'm Mistress's dog!

He exits, barking. The men laugh. KATALIN stands and brushes herself down. She takes an apple from the basket, cleans it against her skirt and takes a bite.

KRISTOF: Is it good?

KATALIN: Shrivelled. Like most things here.

She takes another bite.

KRISTOF: You've got a sharp tongue.

KATALIN: Like a snake.

She smiles.

There's poison in me.

SCENE EIGHTEEN

The COUNTESS's chamber. The ladies-in-waiting dress the COUNTESS in her finery.

COUNTESS: Is he still drawn to me?

ILKA: How could he not be, Mistress?

AGOTHA: How could he not?

ILKA: You were beautiful…

AGOTHA: … still am beautiful… *are* beautiful.

The COUNTESS grunts.

ILKA: So beautiful a painting never caught your likeness.

She opens a necklace case and lifts out the jewels. She drapes the jewels around the COUNTESS's neck as ZSOFI puts a ring on the COUNTESS's finger. AGOTHA sprays perfume.

She's nothing.

COUNTESS: No?

ILKA: No. Just a mountain girl.

AGOTHA: Still got the smell of cow shit under her nails.

The COUNTESS laughs.

ILKA: It's true, Mistress. What can she offer him?

COUNTESS: She can offer him her youth.

Beat.

She has youth enough for you all.

She listens.

That's him at the door. I know his step.

AGOTHA and ZSOFI back out of the room. ILKA squeezes the COUNTESS's hand before retiring from the room. GYORGY enters. The COUNTESS turns slowly in her chair.

You came.

GYORGY: You called for me. If you call for me, I come.

COUNTESS: You had a choice.

GYORGY lowers his head.

GYORGY: How can I serve you, Mistress?

COUNTESS: Serve me?

Angrily.

Look at me!

GYORGY raises his head as the COUNTESS stands. She steps out of her gown to reveal a simple slip – she stands in front of GYORGY.

Look at me.

GYORGY turns away.

Am I disgusting to you?

GYORGY: It's not that.

COUNTESS: Then what?

GYORGY: What do you want from me? You want me to look at you… is that all? You want me to touch you? You want me to kiss you?

He bows his head.

I'll do all these things.

COUNTESS: Because you want it?

GYORGY: Because you ask it.

SCENE NINETEEN

Outside, in the apple orchard. GYORGY urinates against a wall. KATALIN enters.

KATALIN: Put that thing away.

GYORGY: Thought I was alone.

KATALIN: You're not.

Embarrassed, GYORGY shakes himself off and pulls up his trousers. KATALIN marks out a line in the dirt with the toe of her shoe.

GYORGY: What's that for?

He steps forward.

KATALIN: You can't cross.

GYORGY: Why not?

KATALIN: It's a magical line.

GYORGY: No such thing as magic.

Beat.

Why is it magic?

KATALIN: Because I've made it magic.

She murmurs an incantation under her breath.

GYORGY: What are you whispering?

KATALIN: Can't you feel the magic?

GYORGY: I can't feel anything.

KATALIN: The magic tells me things.

GYORGY: Like what?

KATALIN: Like… are you brave and true of heart?

She smiles.

Or are you a man?

GYORGY: You're not magic.

KATALIN: I knew you'd be an unbeliever.

GYORGY laughs.

I'm witch, deep down… I make babies disappear… I'm sin to the core…

GYORGY crosses the line.

325

GYORGY: I believe what I can see with my own eyes. I believe that day turns to night... that night turns to day...

KATALIN: Look at all the stars in the sky, then tell me you still know everything.

She stares up at the sky.

GYORGY: The sky's too big to think about. So I don't think about it.

He takes out a bottle of red liquid and offers it to KATALIN – she holds back.

It's plum brandy.

He smiles.

Why? What did you think it was?

KATALIN scowls. She pulls out the cork and drinks from the bottle.

How old are you?

KATALIN: Where?

She drinks again.

How old I was there and how old I am here... I think they're different questions.

She lifts up the hem of her dress to reveal an ankle.

Here I'm a beautiful child...

She runs her hand up her leg.

... there I was a witch.

She laughs, hitches up her skirts and walks out into the stream.

GYORGY: What are you doing?

KATALIN: My feet are hot.

GYORGY: You can't go out there.

KATALIN: Why not?

GYORGY: If you slip I'm not wading in to pull you out.

KATALIN: Won't you?

She laughs.

So what will you do? Will you stop me if I go further? Will you hold my head above water if I start to drown... or will you push me under?

GYORGY: Have to wait and see, won't you?

KATALIN smiles.

KATALIN: There's wickedness in you.

She wades deeper into the water. GYORGY doesn't know what to do.

GYORGY: Wait!

Muttering, he sits down and pulls off his boots and socks. KATALIN stands and watches.

KATALIN: You've got ugly feet.

GYORGY: Have I?

He rolls up his trousers.

KATALIN: Yes.

GYORGY wades out into the water and KATALIN splashes him.

To match your ugly face.

She laughs.

I knew you'd come... come running.

GYORGY: If you drowned –

KATALIN: What?

Beat.

Were you worried about me… or about what she'd do to you?

They stand, staring at each other. KATALIN laughs nervously.

GYORGY: I had thoughts about you.

KATALIN: What thoughts were those then?

GYORGY: You know.

KATALIN: I don't, so you'll have to tell me.

GYORGY: Are you stupid?

KATALIN: Mother said I was. She was probably right.

GYORGY wades forward and holds KATALIN's head in his hands.

Like what you see?

GYORGY: You've got lines up close.

He runs his fingers slowly over her face.

KATALIN: Lines tell their story.

GYORGY: I'm not interested in your story.

He kisses her – she bites his lip. He pulls away, laughing.

You nearly tore my lip.

KATALIN: If I'd meant to, I would have done.

GYORGY wipes his mouth on the back of his hand.

GYORGY: You're wild.

KATALIN: I've had nobody to break me.

Thunder overhead as rain falls. GYORGY looks up to the castle and turns seriously to KATALIN.

GYORGY: Come out of the stream.

He holds out his hand. KATALIN holds out her hands, then turns them palm-up to the rain.

KATALIN: Is she watching?

GYORGY: She is.

KATALIN: Good. I want her to watch.

She laughs. Music.

SCENE TWENTY

Outside, the rain still falls. GYORGY pulls on his boots.

GYORGY: She'll be angry.

KATALIN: Good. I want her to be angry.

GYORGY: Why?

KATALIN: Because…

She thinks.

… because whatever the reason is that she had me brought here… I want it to be over.

ZSOFI enters with an umbrella and shawl.

ZSOFI: What are you doing out here?

KATALIN laughs. ZSOFI turns to GYORGY.

Was this you?

GYORGY: There's no controlling the girl.

ZSOFI mutters and hurries forward, holding the umbrella over KATALIN's head.

ZSOFI: Come back inside.

KATALIN: I like the rain.

ZSOFI: Inside.

She wraps the shawl around KATALIN's shoulders and leads her inside. GYORGY watches them go.

SCENE TWENTY-ONE

The COUNTESS's chamber. AGOTHA and ILKA rest beside the throne. ZSOFI enters with KATALIN.

KATALIN: You wanted me?

COUNTESS: Yes.

Beat.

Your hair is wet.

ILKA: You'll catch a chill. Are you stupid?

KATALIN turns on her, angrily.

KATALIN: Why do people keep saying that?

ILKA shrinks back.

COUNTESS: Dry your hair by the fire.

KATALIN shakes her head.

KATALIN: It will dry.

She combs her hair with her fingers.

COUNTESS: Come and sit beside me, child.

KATALIN: I'm no child.

She laughs.

I was old in the mountains. I'm young here. Life is strange.

COUNTESS: Sit.

Reluctantly, KATALIN sits beside the COUNTESS.

I was beautiful like you once. My hair was long… my eyes had a sparkle to them. The blood flushed under my skin.

Beat.

How old do you think I am?

KATALIN: I don't know. Do you?

The COUNTESS shrugs.

COUNTESS: I've stopped counting.

KATALIN is unsettled by this comment.

KATALIN: Then you're very old.

COUNTESS: Yes.

Beat.

Turn your face to me.

KATALIN turns.

Why do you look at me like that?

KATALIN: Like what?

COUNTESS: As if you pity me.

She snaps her fingers.

The mirror!

The ladies-in-waiting carry forward a mirror that has been draped in velvet.

331

KATALIN: Why are the mirrors draped?

Beat.

Because you can't see your image in the glass?

ILKA snorts with laughter.

COUNTESS: It's not that we can't see…

She tugs away the velvet drape.

… it's that we choose not to.

They stare in the mirror at the same time.

I want to tell you there's sadness here.

She holds her hand to her chest.

But there's nothing…

The ladies-in-waiting curtsy as they carry the mirror away.

Anything good in here drained out an age ago.

She grasps KATALIN's face in her hands.

But there was good there once.

Music.

SCENE TWENTY-TWO

The servants stand around the COUNTESS's chamber. KATALIN watches from a chair, engrossed. She eats custard from a glass. The servants wear masks – some are human, some animal. Instruments are played. The COUNTESS sits on her throne, which is pushed around the stage as if it's a carriage, led by RUDI.

COUNTESS: Where are you taking me, Rudi?

RUDI: Out through the forest pass.

COUNTESS: How long before we leave the forest?

RUDI: The light's brighter through the branches of the trees now.

Beat.

There... up ahead.

The servants push the throne slowly.

COUNTESS: Stop!

She points out from the 'carriage'.

I will get out here.

RUDI: As you wish.

The servants stop pushing the throne and RUDI helps the COUNTESS down.

COUNTESS: What is that there? Across the water?

RUDI: A town, Countess.

KATALIN: Do they know you in this place?

COUNTESS: Only that I'm a Countess... a lady of quality.

GABOR steps forward and bows. ILKA and AGOTHA stand behind him, their faces concealed behind fans.

GABOR: Good day, Countess.

COUNTESS: Who are you now?

GABOR: I'm the Burgher of this town.

He bows.

I present my compliments to you, Countess.

COUNTESS: And tell me, who are these young girls?

AGOTHA and ILKA giggle.

GABOR: They are my daughters, Countess. Virgins, both of them.

The daughters fan their faces. NURSE steps forward, still rocking her 'baby'.

NURSE: I raised them up myself, Countess. And a third at the teat…

GABOR: Is there one who takes your fancy?

ILKA bows.

There's a thin one…

AGOTHA steps forward.

… and a fat one.

AGOTHA: The blood runs warm in me, Mistress…

GABOR: *(Low.)* She's none too blessed with brains.

COUNTESS: I'll confide in you, Burgher.

She lowers her voice.

I prefer them that way.

GABOR: Will you eat?

COUNTESS: Yes. And a room for the night.

GABOR laughs and claps his hands together.

GABOR: Meat and wine for our noble guest.

He bows.

You honour us, Countess.

COUNTESS: Bring the girl to my room.

GABOR: Which girl?

COUNTESS: The fat one.

GABOR: As you wish it.

The servants change places to represent the inside of a room above the tavern. A light is held close to the COUNTESS's face. There is a knock at the door.

COUNTESS: Come.

AGOTHA enters.

AGOTHA: My father sent me up to speak with you.

Beat.

Have you eaten?

COUNTESS: I've eaten but I haven't yet fed.

Beat.

What age are you?

AGOTHA: If you please, Countess... seventeen.

A ripple of laughter from the servants.

Shut up!

The COUNTESS stares hard at AGOTHA.

Why do you look at me like that?

Beat.

You've got wolf eyes.

COUNTESS: I was thinking what a good match you'd be for my son.

AGOTHA grins.

AGOTHA: Tell me about him, please.

COUNTESS: He's a handsome boy. The very best of boys.

AGOTHA: I've never known handsome men. But I've read about them in books.

COUNTESS: You read books?

AGOTHA: Have them read to me. It's the same.

She paces the room.

Dark-haired princes with long legs who live in castles… and eat custard and cakes.

COUNTESS: That's what's written.

Beat.

My eyes are bad in this light. Come closer, child.

AGOTHA approaches.

What beautiful hair you have.

She runs her fingers through AGOTHA's hair.

AGOTHA: My sister brushes it out for me. And when there are knots she brushes so hard that my eyes water.

She giggles.

My sister is a bitch.

The COUNTESS pulls back AGOTHA's hair.

COUNTESS: And a beautiful white neck.

AGOTHA: Are you listening to me?

Suddenly, the COUNTESS sinks her teeth into AGOTHA's neck – AGOTHA cries out, pulling red ribbons from her dress to illustrate spurting blood.

Help! Death! Ilka!

ILKA enters the room, in horror.

ILKA: The blood's spurting from her. Father!

The COUNTESS bites into ILKA's neck and as before, it spurts red ribbons. KATALIN is laughing now – enjoying the spectacle.

GABOR: My beautiful, beautiful… stupid daughters!

He wails. The NURSE steps forward and offers up the 'baby' – the COUNTESS steps back in horror. The music falls silent. RUDI attempts to keep the pretence going.

RUDI: The horses are fed and watered.

The COUNTESS allows herself to be led aboard the carriage.

Are you sated, Mistress?

COUNTESS: Never!

Beat.

We must fly from this place.

RUDI: As you wish it.

He holds up his whip.

Hi!

He whips the horses and the carriage is away.

COUNTESS: I'm tired.

She slumps in her chair. The servants stand, motionless.

KATALIN: She's not well.

ZSOFI hurries forward.

ZSOFI: Are you sick?

ILKA: She looks sick.

AGOTHA: What's wrong with her?

ILKA: Is she close to death, do you think?

ZSOFI: Death would be a blessing.

AGOTHA: What's a blessing?

COUNTESS: I'm fearful of death. I'm fearful of life. And here I sit, trapped somewhere between the two.

ZSOFI takes a step forward.

ZSOFI: You're not well, madam.

COUNTESS: I'm not sick…

ZSOFI: But, Mistress –

COUNTESS: I'm not sick and I'm not well. I'm not mad, and I'm not in my right mind. I'm not this and I'm not that.

ZSOFI: I've got your medicine.

COUNTESS: I don't want medicine.

She pulls ZSOFI close.

Don't do this.

ZSOFI: You know what will happen.

The COUNTESS struggles. ZSOFI takes out the syringe. KATALIN gets up from her seat but RUDI gently holds her back.

KATALIN: You're hurting her!

ZSOFI: Hold her down.

The ladies-in-waiting restrain the COUNTESS.

KATALIN: Let go of her!

ZSOFI flicks the syringe.

COUNTESS: No!

ZSOFI clutches the syringe between her teeth. She rolls up the COUNTESS's sleeve and ties cord around her arm.

AGOTHA: Don't be a child. Take your medicine.

KATALIN: I said… let go!

AGOTHA strikes KATALIN. ZSOFI injects the syringe and the COUNTESS screams out.

ILKA: There… there… ssh.

She smooths back the COUNTESS's hair.

AGOTHA: You're all better now.

COUNTESS: Better?

Beat.

Leave me.

ILKA: But, Mistress –

AGOTHA: Mistress –

COUNTESS: Get out!

Music.

SCENE TWENTY-THREE

ILKA walks with KATALIN to the COUNTESS's chamber.

ILKA: She won't take her medicine.

KATALIN: What makes you think she'll listen to me?

ILKA: I don't think that.

They enter the COUNTESS's chamber. The COUNTESS looks diminished now, smaller, as if sucked dry.

COUNTESS: Katalin.

She gasps for air as KATALIN approaches the throne.

KATALIN: Don't speak.

COUNTESS: Hear… me…

Beat.

There were riches here once. Gold… and silver… and jewels enough to trickle through my fingers.

ILKA: The jewels went to bribe the aldermen and burghers.

The COUNTESS smiles at the memory.

So they'd send their daughters to the castle.

COUNTESS: But now we enact hollow rituals.

She looks around her.

It's a half-life. I am the queen bee dying in the hive.

She coughs.

KATALIN: There is medicine.

COUNTESS: No!

She pulls her wrap around her.

I have lived lifetimes beyond my lifetime.

The COUNTESS takes KATALIN's hand.

And life palls.

Beat.

In the mountains… in the forests… in the towns and villages… don't let them pity the old…

She squeezes KATALIN's hand tightly.

… make them fear us.

SCENE TWENTY-FOUR

The solarium. The COUNTESS enters, leaning heavily on a cane, her eyes hidden behind dark glasses. She wears a fur wrap around her shoulders. VIDOR walks with the COUNTESS, carrying a candle.

COUNTESS: I don't know these hands now… the skin like parchment. Bloodless.

Beat.

Imagine that? To not know my own hands.

VIDOR: You've grown old.

COUNTESS: Yes.

VIDOR: We've all grown old.

COUNTESS: You were always old.

There is a low growl in the darkness.

Dog? Dog, is that you in the shadows?

An answering whine from DOG.

Bring me more light.

DOG carries the candle forward.

Good dog.

The COUNTESS smoothes his hair. DOG utters a low, appreciative growl.

Faithful dog.

DOG: Mistress.

COUNTESS: The clocks are running slow.

ILKA whimpers in the shadows.

Ilka…

ILKA shakes her head.

… come.

Wiping her eyes, ILKA walks forward.

Here…

She slips the jewelled ring from her finger.

… take this.

ILKA: But, Mistress –

Gently, the COUNTESS pushes the ring into ILKA's hand. ILKA kisses the ring and slips it into a pocket of her dress. The COUNTESS waves her away. ILKA exits, bobbing her head

VIDOR: Are you ready?

COUNTESS: Yes.

She cups her hand around the candle and extinguishes the flame – the room is plunged into darkness. VIDOR turns a large wooden handle and the shutters are loudly opened back – light pours into the solarium. The COUNTESS laughs, dropping her wrap. She stands in the full glare of the sun. She takes off the glasses and blinks in the light. A sound comes from inside her – a roar.

SCENE TWENTY-FIVE

Music. Almost as a coronation, the ladies-in-waiting group together around the throne, working busily. They step back to reveal KATALIN, dressed in the COUNTESS's jewels and finery. DOG has curled up on the floor. The servants have gathered in the shadows. ILKA bows to KATALIN.

KATALIN: Rudi…

RUDI steps forward.

… let there be blood!

RUDI kisses KATALIN's hand and hurries away. There is a cry of approval from the servants.

End.

WWW.OBERONBOOKS.COM

Follow us on Twitter @oberonbooks
& Facebook @OberonBooksLondon